Da Capo BEST MUSIC WRITING 2005

Da Capo BEST MUSIC WRITING 2005

The Year's Finest Writing on Rock, Hip-Hop, Jazz, Pop, Country, & More

JT LeRoy
GUEST EDITOR

Paul Bresnick
SERIES EDITOR

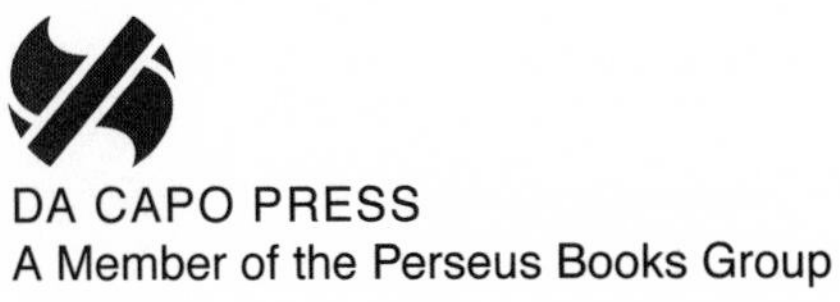

DA CAPO PRESS
A Member of the Perseus Books Group

List of credits/permissions for all pieces can be found on page 201.

Set in 10.5 point Janson Text by the Perseus Books Group

Cataloging-in-Publication data for this book is available from the Library of Congress.

First Da Capo Press edition 2005
ISBN-13 978-0-306-81446-4
ISBN-10 0-306-81446-3

Published by Da Capo Press
A Member of the Perseus Books Group
www.dacapopress.com

1 2 3 4 5 6 7 8 9—08 07 06 05

Dedicated to the joyous memory of Henry Flesh, who is flyin' in the heavens playin' geetar with his teeth and toes!

"Once you're more in touch with human vulnerability, especially your own, you become less concerned to censor and condemn the ignorant armies and more to nurture the values in which you continue to have faith, however wavering. . . . You may even come to recognize writing as an aspect of wise living and poems [and songs—JT] not as summit or vanguard but as part of some larger, more humbling tale."

—Fay Zwicky, VAN GOGH's EAR,
BEST WORLD POETRY & PROSE #4

CONTENTS

Introduction

Better Than Anything I Could Say

I am a fuckin' lemming (not like the Motörhead kind, though I do have days when I am. But usually I am Angus Young, in the schoolboy shorts too). Anyway, I stand before you like many hath afore me and say ok, well, what the fuck right do I have to arbitrate anything about music?

I mean you'd fuckin' hope an editor of a science journal could at least tell an atom from a, uh, ya know, another thing that floats around that is small. Or check out any book review section; 'tis rare they assign a review of the latest Jefferson biography to a food critic. But there are those of us writer types who reckon because we get into, and I mean intensely dig blown-up photos of mitochondria, we have the right not only to party with them atom splitters but also to pose commentary over their shoulders. It's fuckin' madness, ya gotta admit. Madness, I tell you. I mean would I, not comprehending any of the rules of football, be allowed anywhere near the locker room (well, that would be for other reasons) or be invited to be an outfielder, umpire, or goalie? Ya know what I mean?

So back to me being Lemmy . . . I recently called a publicist to get a copy of an upcoming CD I wanted to write about. The publicist knew my name, so I avoided that 12-year-old-trying-to-scam-free-records thing, but she said she didn't know I wrote about music.

I gasped in horror, "But, but, but that's how I started . . . "

I'm all about the music, man. . . .

"Uh, howdy, uh, hello, uh . . . ?" (They can hear my heartbeat, they know I am an outlier.)

"Pub . . . Bliss. . . City."

"Hi, yeah, uh, I . . . writer . . . Me mean . . . I write for . . . " (check notes).

"Hold, please." (Loud music roars over phone, covers my heartbeat . . . that is good.)

"Yes . . . Hel-low?"

"Yeah, uh, um . . . yeah" (Hoist my neck up and away from the chest, she can still hear that thumping, I am not a drummer. I am a writer, writers do not pound, right?) "I am Terminator and I write for *NY Press*. . . . "

"*Terminator?*" (Shrill laughter) "Whom do you wish to speak to, *Terminator*?"

"Uh, I'd like to speak to God . . . ha ha ha ha . . . " (Guttural clearing of throat. I will be shot before dawn.) "Just, just kidding. Uh, Billy C-C-C-Corgan?"

"Dream on, kid, and you're not getting any free fucking product either."

CLICK . . .

Much like a pistol in a proper duel, the breath is drawn from the other end of the phone. 'Tis such a command of inhalation, the petite hairs of my eustachian tube yearn toward it religiously. And I marvel at the vast landscapes contained within this inhalation quickly unraveling before me, the gleaming ramparts that thousands of sad and lonely (can they be anything but? I think not) fanzine makers have attempted to traverse, only to land on blistering plains mined with burrowed porcupines. Here, their crucified but quaint limbs have been abandoned, their ink and staple-blemished fingers bring a fragile tear to my eye. Oh, but further ahead, thrusting upward, is a field of melted stalks of digital tape recorders, crooked from a hiding sun. I gasp within the tail end of this lungful of air; I am swallowed into the land of the misbegotten, to slink past the barely quiescent winged dragon only to have to dig through mafia-approved concrete with a plastic shovel for the desired chalice, only to have their bones crunched and munched within the jaws of the Assistant to the Publicist, ground into a special fiber that makes those extra-heavy vinyl record releases still possible.

Requests must always be faxed, signed by your third grade teacher, and made holy by the sons of York. Then they go right into the recycling bin. But having an editor who will vouch for you is always helpful.

How many APB-type calls did John Strausbaugh, my very first editor, have to field?

"Uh, John, we got a 12-year-old girl who can barely string together a coherent sentence, claiming she writes for you, she wants to interview Rancid. . . . "

"Yup, that would be Terminator," was his always amused reply. "*He's* 17, but 12 fits just fine."

Writer Bruce Benderson had written a story about me for *NY Press*, accompanied by a story I wrote. After the piece ran, the valiant editor Strausbaugh asked, "Ya wanna write for us, kiddo?"

"Uh, yeah." I wasn't sure he was serious.

"The pay . . . well, you'll have to pay us . . . just kidding, but not kidding by that much."

"What, uh, what can I write for you?" I gasped.

"Got more of them stories?"

I did, but I knew they weren't ready. I knew my writing was like an infant in some Philip K. Dick uterus I could see into; I was still undergoing mitosis, organs still finding proper milieu. . . .

"I, uh, really am into music. . . . "

"Music, eh? You want to interview bands for us, musicians?"

"Ok . . . I mean yes, sir, I do."

"Good. Terminator, you got yourself a job. But I want some more of those stories sometime. . . . "

And this is how it usually went down: Pitch John, and if he said ok, I faxed my request and made the follow-up calls. But I could always identify the swoosh particular to a publicists' eyes as they roll with immense velocity. Think of a cartoon window shade.

"Uh, John, I need you to call publicity again, they still don't believe me."

"Heck, I don't believe you, Terminator. You write for me? What are you, 11?" Reassuring deep chest laugh. "I'm on it." He'd grab his staff and part the waters of snide publicists for me, and I would get access to the artist.

After a year of writing for the *NY Press*, I was amazed that so many musicians were kinda like idiot savants. Gorgeous music, but the brilliant lyrics seemed to be an accident or broadcast in from some frequency only musicians can hear. Like Bob Dylan says in the *LA Times* interview with Robert Hilburn included in this collection, "It's like a ghost writing a song like that. It gives you the song and it goes away . . . You don't know what it means. Except the ghost picked me to write the song."

Most of the punks I was around as a kid were readers. Even the hardcore junkie punks. Otherwise you didn't know the ideology you were spouting, the meaning of the CRASS or other symbol you wore. You then were guilty of the most grievous sin of being a PUNK, and that was being just a fucking *poseur*, into it for the fashion.

Sometimes I'd interview musicians, and they were very present with me, offering deeper responses than what I'd read in their press releases. They didn't laugh at me or my quirky questions. They just let themselves be unguarded, and we talked literature, music, and the worlds they knew. And with some of them it felt as if they hoisted me on their shoulders, revealing to me the vistas visible from the vantage point of connecting with millions, the rarefied brown M&M-reeking air of being an artist. They lent me their breathing masks, I stayed in contact with those artists, and they helped me get back to my stories.

In the meantime I had become addicted to reading REAL music writers. I sought out Greil Marcus (whose essay on Buddy Holly, the first hipster geek, graces these pages) and the whole OG crew. I religiously read the writers from *The New York Times* to the *Village Voice* to *Rolling Stone* to the *LA Times*. For some, I was forced to sit in the library with a dictionary and encyclopedia to come close to comprehending what I was reading. And I wanted to comprehend. I was spellbound, the same way I was spellbound by reading Bruno Bettelheim's *Uses of Enchantment*, to learn the under-language of why some fairy tales spoke to our particular story, which was what these music writers do. They explain, and I was also amazed at how music writing is *not* necessary for one to appreciate a piece of music, a song, a whole genre, but it can trick out meaning and layers that make it *feel* necessary. Like when I'm reading Chaucer or Shakespeare, I can see what's there, but having notes that explain the details of the language, placing it in context, adds a whole other realm. And I came to realize how many musicians write from a universal unconscious. They are hitting on a culture's themes, and usually it is not best for them to try and explain what they did, 'coz they don't even fucking know. It's the music writer's job to tell us. And I got very addicted to trying to understand why, why that Clash song "London Calling" did something to me; it takes Sasha Frere-Jones's excellent *New Yorker* piece "1979" to explain it to me in a historical social-political context, 'coz I didn't get that kind of learning. I grew up reading old fanzines, *Flipside*, *Maximum Rock 'N' Roll*, *Touch & Go*, which for me contained a punk revolution beyond the confines of a sad family landscape. Someone always had a collection under the bed, often protected in Piggly Wiggly's plastic vegetable bags. In those pages I would read about the beefs of scene battles, straight edge vs. gutter punks vs. Crass punks, the skinhead movements, analysis of the history of it all fought passionately on theoretical fields. I first read about Nietzsche in these 'zines. Like it says on John Peel's tombstone and in the Undertones' song "Teenage dreams are hard to beat." But lately, so much music writing is just solid smack talking. I dig pop culture, but man, I am shocked by how little time we got for serious, artful, crafted, music writing. So much of what I culled through for this book taught me how much music writing now is really gossip reporting, shit talking, no fucking different from one of those after-dinner TV exposés on the underside of celebrity. They had it all, used drugs, were a tad unhinged (show us an artist that fuckin' isn't), jail, death of a lady, bad bad times, but maybe they came back after destroying how many lives? After they got out of jail, they played a show or cut a record, making this a story of redemption, not gossip. And though the writing is very fucking crafted and I could barely lift my eyes from the bloodspatter portrayed on the page, it did not make me feel noble, or elevated, or give me deeper understanding, which is what I want from my music writing. Like "The Shortwave and the Calling," David Segal's amazing piece on ambient shortwave radio spy music and Wilco's somewhat underhanded appropriation of same for their album titled *Yankee Hotel Foxtrot*, I want music writing to be the illuminating footnotes to Chaucer and Shakespeare. I want it to be Boswell to the dictionary man. Music writing, when done with sheer brilliance, can do what a song can—fucking explain, or open another realm, like OG Robert Christgau does in his deep discussion of the racial minefield of minstrelsy, "In Search of Jim Crow."

And snark is the new black, and that is why I didn't pick any of those articles. They won't stand the test of time. Why would a magazine allow a music writer to exercise his or her craft to reflect on an artist when it can just sneer 'em down. Which leads me to reference the very cool Kalefa Sanneh's "The Rap Against Rockism" piece contained within. I'm Carrie White at this prom, and this piece is a very swell latching of the gymnasium doors. You ain't getting out that easy. . . .

Maybe it was the betrayal of Kurt. Kurt was the last of the tooth fairies for a whole generation of us. Ya find out about Santa, the Easter Bunny, but ya still got that fuckin' tooth fairy to give you hope. He was one that a lot of us willingly and unself-consciously went along with, gave ourselves over to.

And then he betrayed us believers.

I remember he made it seem so doable, the same way he made being a musician who was honest seem like an achievable goal. Suicide, you can just do it, like the Nike ads say. And for those of us he left behind who didn't give up, didn't follow his example, what's left to say when you lose a key to the magical kingdom? The king is dead, long live snark, be it dead or alive. Chris Norris's "The Ghost of Saint Kurt" helped me forgive him, or forgive myself for not following him. So back to what gives me the right to be here. What follows is an excerpt from an interview the writer Mary Gaitskill did with the band Radiohead in *Alternative Press*, April 1998. Mary was a friend, as well as a writing mentor to me. We talked about everything. I was still Terminator, my nom de plum, and still learning to give hum to the mess inside. She told me how she'd been stuck in the interview with Thom Yorke and about how she told him how I'd used his songs to communicate in my therapy. I think that was one of the most pivotal forces in my desire to interview musicians. I knew I didn't have any significant, new, or erudite way of adding to the canon of musical critiques. I just know music allows me, like millions of others, a framework to filter my emotions through, and I really just want to say thank you.

> Backstage, the journalist approaches Yorke with a smile on her face. "That was a beautiful show."
>
> "Thank you," he says, smiling back. "Sorry about the other day," he adds. . . .
>
> "It seemed like you were being mean," she says.
>
> "Oh, I was. But it seemed like you were doing this heavy literary thing, and I didn't like it. But then I realized it wasn't like that."
>
> She hesitates. "I know you don't like to deal with emotional stuff," she says, "so you don't have to deal with this, but there's this friend of mine who's 17, and your music had a really good emotional effect on him."
>
> "Seventeen?" Yorke smiles even more. "Really?" He can sneer like a bastard, but when he smiles, he looks like a 17-year-old himself.
>
> "Yeah. I know him because he's a writer." She tells about this friend, who was a street hustler from the ages of 13 to 15. His mom was a drug addict who sometimes turned tricks with him, and who ultimately abandoned him in a hotel with an older man. Through a public clinic, he got hooked up with a psychiatrist who basically saved him—although it took a while.

"He didn't know how to deal with the psychiatrist at first," she continues. "He couldn't talk to him. So he played him your record, *The Bends*, and they talked about that. It's how they bonded—your record was how they were slowly able to get into other subjects."

She doesn't add that the kid (a raw talent who writes under the name Terminator) said the record expressed feelings he had but didn't know how to convey. But what she does say is also true: "He doesn't think you're responsible for his feelings. He's smart. He doesn't expect you to make the same music on every record, even if it was really important to him. And he wouldn't care what somebody wrote about it in a magazine. Your fans probably don't either. The magazine article is just somebody talking. Even if it's interesting, it's just a frill, it's the music that counts."

"That's great," says Yorke. "You should write that. That's better than anything I could say."

JT LeRoy
June 2005
San Francisco

INGRID SISCHY AND CAMILLE PAGLIA

From the Editor's Desk

A Conversation Between Ingrid Sischy and Camille Paglia

INGRID SISCHY: **It's our annual music issue, so I thought it would be good to talk about a subject you've been interested in for a long time: rock-star style. Take it away.**

CAMILLE PAGLIA: Well, from the moment rock 'n' roll was born in the 1950s, most aspiring rock stars modeled themselves on Elvis Presley: the brooding rebel in proletarian blue jeans, half hipster, half hood, like Marlon Brando and James Dean. But by the mid-1960s, when I was in college, the British mod trend had turned rock stars into dandies. It was a rejection of the corporate gray-flannel suits of the conformist 1950s. Young men grew their hair long and started experimenting with fine fabrics and bright colors—silks and velvets, Indian paisley patterns, flowing scarves like Jim Hendrix's pink feather boa. From American hippies came beaded necklaces and Navajo silver bracelets and turquoise rings. That was the great high glamour moment of rock-star fashion, which went from the late '60s to the mid-'70s, when young men were strutting like peacocks.

IS: **It was also totally plugged into the sexual revolution.**

CP: Yes. It wasn't just women who were suddenly liberated by the pill. Most rock stars were ostentatiously heterosexual, but there was a strongly androgynous and homoerotic quality to their self-presentation in that period, which remains a template for musicians today. Rock stars are always defining themselves either for or against the template. For instance, Lenny Kravitz, like Prince in the '80s, is constantly channeling '60s style.

IS: What about women rock stars of that era, like Janis Joplin?

CP: Janis Joplin was an oddity, a Texas blues singer fronting a San Francisco acid-rock band. Her style was eclectic and bizarre, a kind of slatternly, New Orleans hooker look with Moroccan fabrics and backless harem slippers. It was almost Jean Harlowesque—a ripe, womanly thing that was out of sync with contemporary fashion.

IS: Who else?

CP: Patti Smith was totally revolutionary as a sexual persona. Unlike Grace Slick and Marianne Faithfull, she was a major gender bender, modeling herself on her idol (and mine), Keith Richards: tough, scrawny, ravaged. In Robert Mapplethorpe's stunning photo for her 1975 debut album, *Horses*, she's wearing a man's tie and draping a suit jacket over her shoulder like Frank Sinatra.

IS: Deborah Harry?

CP: A brilliant singer! What crystal clarity and perfect emotional pitch. In the '70s, Blondie turned rock retro. After all the grandiosity of arena rock and message-heavy protest songs, rock returned to its simple, peppy pop origins to refresh itself. As a performer, Harry also looked backwards to reappropriate pre-feminist images like Marilyn Monroe but with the avant-garde irony of the Velvet Underground and Andy Warhol milieu. There's a direct line from Harry to Belinda Carlisle of the Go-Go's, who also jumped back to the '50s: "We're going to be like cheerleaders and beauty-pageant contestants and sorority queens!" In one video, they're even zipping around on water skis. Fashion-wise, Belinda Carlisle as a spunky, bratty blonde was the crucial transition between Debbie Harry and Madonna in the '80s.

IS: What's so interesting about the '60s and '70s is that what was going on socially and politically merged with what was going on visually and stylistically. So the style embodied the sexual revolution, the gay revolution, and the civil rights revolution.

CP: Yes, it was a cultural explosion that transformed music. Thanks to Bob Dylan, rock was cross-fertilized with folk music, with its cutting edge social issues. The Beatles' first albums were all about girls and teenage heartbreak, but once they met Dylan, John Lennon began writing lyrics with searing social consciousness.

IS: And then there were the album covers that emerged at the time. It was a new kind of folk art.

CP: It was tremendous. Most album covers from the '50s were boring and generic. Then, all of a sudden, boom! Sixties album covers were scrutinized by my generation as if they were holy writ—like David Bailey's gritty photos of the sullen, pockmarked Rolling Stones. Rock stars now began to think about image, fashion, packaging.

IS: But some '50s album covers were fantastic too—like the Blue Note jazz series. It was a dynamic moment in graphics and typefaces. For me, truthfully, some of that '60s psychedelia stuff got kind of tedious after a while.

CP: Everything becomes a cliché. But at the start, it was incredible—the surrealistic album covers of the Beatles' *Revolver* [1966] and Cream's *Disraeli Gears* [1967] or the distorted fish-eye lens cover of Jimi Hendrix's first album [*Are You Experienced?*, 1967]. Rock poster art was also innovative, reviving the late–19th century graphic styles of Alphonse Mucha, Henri de Toulouse-Lautrec, and Aubrey Beardsley. Tiffany and Lalique also had a comeback, thanks mainly to gay connoisseurs. So there was this strange confluence of the psychedelic '80s with art nouveau and fin de siècle aestheticism and decadence, the Edwardian look of the 1890s. The pioneering fashion synthesis came out of London, where young artsy types were pillaging antique-clothing stores along Portobello Road. It was a mind-boggling fashion fantasia: People mixed and matched clothes like costumes, whether it was a violet pin-striped Edwardian suit or a brass-buttoned pea coat and sailor's bell-bottoms from military surplus. And then there were the futuristic, geometric mod outfits coming from Carnaby Street. It was one of the great fashion moments of the 20th century.

Think of Jimmy Page, the genius guitarist of Led Zeppelin. He was a gorgeous vision onstage—a slight-looking, longhaired fellow wielding a guitar like a machine gun. He wore magnificent, sleekly form-fitting black suits embroidered with occult astrological emblems of the moon and stars. The new style for men was plunging necklines that exposed the bare chest. Mick Jagger also wore skimpy, skintight jumpsuits that showed off his taut, hairless torso.

IS: As you touched on a moment ago, it was a moment when photography's role in music was intrinsic to the excitement. What was the first photo on an album cover that made an impact on you?

CP: It was definitely the first Beatles major-label release in the U.S., called *Meet the Beatles!* [1964], with Robert Freeman's stark photo of the Beatles in black turtlenecks with their faces half in shadow. I remember standing on the street gaping at it in the Woolworth's window in Syracuse. I was absolutely thunderstruck—it bore no relationship whatever to prior images of pop singers like Fabian and Frankie Avalon, pretty boys with pink, airbrushed cheeks. Rock albums and posters became religious icons to us in the '60s. In college and grad school and even at my first teaching job at Bennington, my walls were completely plastered with rock posters! They were high-contrast, black-and-white images taken with small 35mm cameras.

IS: Mostly by unknown photographers.

CP: Yes! You'd go into poster shops in Greenwich Village and buy those things for $2.95. They were true works of art. The quality of pop posters today is appalling—mediocre images poorly reproduced. Young people today have little or no contact with good photography.

IS: Well, I think there's as much good photography as there ever was. But with music the presentation form has changed to small CDs. Now so much visual creativity goes into music videos. But photography deserves some of the credit for why music and musicians made such an impact on fashion and style in the second half of the 20th century. Do you think there are parallel strong fashion statements emerging from today's rock stars?

CP: I'm not impressed.

IS: Look, you have Britney Spears totally done up for a video, but when you actually see her as she is in life, photographed at the airport or on the street, she looks just like any mall rat. She's not completing the image she presents on film, not following through.

CP: It shows the gigantic gap between Britney and Madonna, who has always had a superb instinct for the still photograph. Madonna's career is much more than dance music and sensational videos: It's also a phenomenal series of still images. Britney Spears, a leading disciple in the Madonna dynasty, doesn't understand any of this!

IS: But to me, today there are certain contemporary musicians who do manage to have an all-around strong visual image and strong style. One who immediately comes to mind is Eminem, who has as clear-eyed a statement of style as anybody in the past. It's a look that translates from his videos to his public appearances to his life.

CP: People generally view Eminem as a rapper trying to blend with black culture, but I classify him with the punks—the street-boy and juvenile-delinquent look that goes back to Iggy Pop and the groundbreaking but short-lived group Television, whom I feel lucky to have seen perform at CBGB's in the '70s. The Sex Pistols, with their spiky hair and torn T-shirts, were later imitators who fell flat in the U.S. Kurt Cobain's grunge look, emerging from the Pacific Northwest, would be a further variation of that.

IS: Let's take another contemporary of Eminem's: Jay-Z. What's so interesting about his man-about-town style is that it fights the cliché of the rapper with the pants falling down.

CP: Yes, and I'd add P. Diddy, with his Sean Jean line inspired by Savile Row tailoring, and the wittily flamboyant André 3000 of OutKast to the very short list of those trying to revise the now tiresome formulas of hip-hop—the boxy, bulky silhouette and adolescent sports logos. Performers looking for something new are turning retro again.

IS: In that context, I'm going to throw another name at you: Gwen Stefani.

CP: I take her very seriously. She's smart and savvy and has an eye for fashion in the Madonna way. Her style has evolved from a scampy California-punk look to a dreamy evocation of studio-era Hollywood figures like Jean Harlow and Dorothy Lamour.

IS: And she's playing Harlow, of course, in Martin Scorsese's upcoming movie about Howard Hughes, *The Aviator*. Okay, Beyoncé.

CP: Beyoncé strikes me as a very centered personality who gives off a kind of warm, Rita Hayworth feeling—a statuesque womanliness, a dignified reserve even in the midst of exhibitionistic sensuality. She holds herself with great presence, and I've never seen her in anything she doesn't wear well, including that mane of hair, which she whips around onstage to great effect.

IS: In the last few years, she and Jennifer Lopez have done a lot for what our mothers used to call "meat on the bones."

CP: Well, Jennifer Lopez single-handedly injected the eroticism of large, shapely buttocks into mainstream Anglo-American taste. Before that, it was primarily confined to black and Latino culture.

IS: And with that Lopez put the spotlight on the view from the back, which gives us a good transition to the idea of looking back. Let's focus on the recent past. It's giving this time a certain tone, isn't it?

CP: I think we're in a period of comfort and reassurance rather than innovation in style. This is post–9/11, and people don't want their buttons pushed.

IS: I think the opposite, if you start to feel the mood sweeping across this country with all these pockets of resistance to the Iraq war and to Bush, and if we look at the role that music played the last time around—with the Vietnam War—in the '60s and '70s. The audience is waiting for those figures of protest to emerge again.

CP: But I worry that young people may be jaded by the low-level popular culture that has blanketed them for their entire lives. It's become their social environment, which they're forced to adapt to. They don't have direct contact, as we did, with the powerful, subversive traditions of blues, folk music, and Beat poetry. Another problem is that they lack a clear-cut sense of generation: '60s dissidents bonded against the authoritarian '50s.

IS: **But you do feel a yearning in the young.**

CP: Absolutely. I think there's a yearning for truth, a desire to find great fundamentals again. The next big voice who changes everything is going to be someone who can absorb the past but also speak to the moment. Reality is extremely traumatic right now. You wonder how a nascent artist in his or her adolescence can psychologically process a culture that's so split between the hedonistic carnival of pop and the horrors of terrorism and war—skyscrapers incinerated, bodies dragged through streets, hostages decapitated. There was a similar crisis during World War II, but Americans were much more united. War is always a mutilating and brutalizing experience, so perhaps this generation of young people will be creatively delayed. We might not hear from their strongest voices until they're in their late twenties or thirties. My advice is never to lose will and aspiration. If young people feel dwarfed, eclipsed, or silenced by our omnipresent commercial culture, they should model themselves on marathon runners—keep observing, keep storing up experience, and speak later.

IS: **And the beauty of pop culture is that there's always the possibility that tomorrow we'll wake up and all these new ideas will have burst forth.**

CP: Exactly. The seeds are being planted now.

MICHAEL CORCORAN

1979 Calling

What is that?

I kept wondering about the strange disco music with the guys talking over the beat that I'd been hearing all over Manhattan since stepping off a Greyhound bus a few hours earlier. I couldn't go two blocks without hearing "a hip hop the hippie the hippie to the hip hop, a you don't stop" from cars, from radios, from apartment windows. "The rock it to the bang bang boogie, say up jumped the boogie, to the rhythm of the boogie, to the beat." That song was as omnipresent as the sound of honking taxis, as thick in the air as steam from the subway grates.

The roots of rap have been traced to World War II rhymes like "Jody the Grinder," the Last Poets, Muhammad Ali and Jamaican toasting, but nothing heard previously could prepare one for the first exposure to recorded hip-hop music. In September 1979, the Big Apple sounded like outer space.

I was at the intersection of 14th Street and Third Avenue, standing in line outside the Palladium, when I heard that song again. A trio of black kids passed by, one carrying what appeared to be a black suitcase with speakers, and as they strutted to the groove, I asked someone in line, "What is that?"

"It's called rap music," the guy said. Rap music? Better write that down.

Just five days earlier, Sugarhill Records had released "Rapper's Delight," the Big Bang of hip-hop, and New York was under siege to the sound.

But I had other things on my mind than a 14-minute novelty record enjoying what I presumed to be a brief time of notoriety. I had come to New York from Albany, three hours upstate, to see the Clash, a British punk band on a political mission, who spiced their socialistic snarl with doses of rebel-rousing reggae. More musically proficient than the Ramones, deeper than the Sex Pistols, the Clash, dubbed "the only band that matters," made the record industry take punk seriously.

When they emerged onstage at the Palladium that Friday night, the Clash didn't look like revolutionaries, but rock stars, especially guitarist Mick Jones in his red shirt and black leather pants. They opened with a trio of trademark fast, angry numbers—"Safe European Home," "I'm So Bored with the U.S.A." and "Complete Control"—but then they went into a song that sounded unlike the others. "Here's one from our next record," singer Joe Strummer announced, as Jones played the now familiar fat guitar chords and sideman Mickey Gallagher laid heavy on the keyboards. "London calling to the faraway towns / Now war is declared, a battle come down / London calling to the underworld / Come out of your cupboards you boys and girls," Strummer sang in his cluttered voice.

The typically jaded and sedate New York audience sat back down and stayed in their seats until the very end, when the band encored with the punk anthems "Career Opportunities" and "White Riot" and there were scattered pockets of ecstasy. Frustrated with the crowd's complacency, especially in response to such material as "Clampdown," "Wrong 'Em Boyo" and "Guns of Brixton," which the band had spent the previous two months recording, bassist Paul Simonon smashed his guitar on the stage; a photo of the moment before impact provided the cover art of "London Calling," which would come out like a big stylistic boundary eraser three months later.

I wish I could say I was aware that I had been standing at a major musical—and cultural—crossroads that day in New York when I first heard rap music and songs from "London Calling." The truth is that I had no idea hip-hop would become much more than the year's "Disco Duck" or that the Clash was about to give punk rock its "Exile on Main Street." As I spent the night at Danceteria (cheaper than a hotel room), I was thinking that if not for stellar opening sets by the Undertones ("the Irish Ramones") and soul greats Sam & Dave, the Clash concert would've been disappointing. And when the Danceteria DJ played "Rapper's Delight," I was already sick of it.

Who knew that 1979 would be a pivotal year, creating sparks that would engulf pop culture 25 years later? Who could foresee that the minority would so soon become the majority, that the menacing would one day be mainstream, that rap music would grow into a $10 billion a year industry, that punk bands would sell out stadiums? At the exact midpoint, 25 years on each side, between the Elvis explosion and today, 1979 was a wax paper year, separating two distinctly different cultural cuts of meat. On one side you had Kid Creole and the Coconuts, Gloria Gaynor, "Comes a Time." On the other you had Prince, Madonna, "Rust Never Sleeps." It was the start of a new edgy era of risk and adventure.

Any rattling off of the banner years of music includes 1954, the birth of rock; 1977, when punk broke; and 1991's Nirvana arrival. You'll rarely hear 1979 mentioned as a musical watershed moment because the year's effect was not sudden, but rather at a time release pace. In 1979, rap and punk polarized fans, which was part of the appeal, just as preachers railing against "the devil's music" in the 1950s helped build Graceland. Show me a style of music the majority of adults hate, and I'll show you a line of kids around the block. But you had to wonder just how long talking records and angry guitars would keep attracting new rebels.

But the forms kept evolving, artistically, with hip-hop going from nonsensical boasts to message music that Public Enemy leader Chuck D likened to CNN for the black community. Just as the Clash added textures to their sound when they grew as musicians, former punk bands including Talking Heads, U2 and R.E.M. expanded on "three chords and the truth" with broader musical statements, attracting fans who, in previous generations, might've clung to safer choices.

The connection between rap and punk, two completely different-sounding forms of music, goes back to their beginnings in the broke-down neighborhoods of New York City in the summer of 1974. That's when a Jamaican-born DJ nicknamed Kool Herc hired MCs to hype up the crowds at his block parties in the South Bronx. Using the same do-it-yourself mode, a quartet of leather-jacketed punks who called themselves the Ramones played their first gig at Bowery dive CBGB around the same time.

The genres were both invented by poor people disenfranchised by the big musical trends of the day—disco and arena rock. "And You Don't Stop: 30 Years Of Hip Hop," a fascinating five-part VH1 documentary airing Monday through Friday, starts by detailing the five years before rap was recorded, when blacks and Puerto Ricans from the burned-out South Bronx couldn't afford to get into the big Manhattan discos, so they made their own dance parties, hot-wiring street lamps to power massive sound systems in city parks.

White city kids, meanwhile, couldn't relate to the satin-covered bloat of mid-'70s rock bands, with their feathered hair and phony mystical lyrics, so they bought pawn shop guitars and learned just enough chords to set their everyday lives to music.

In their earliest years, rap and punk were strictly underground, unlikely to break out of the basement or the block party. Nobody made a rap record until 1979, because no one thought of committing those crowd-stroked party jams to vinyl. When "King Tim III," the first rap recording, was released a couple weeks before "Rapper's Delight," it was relegated to the B-side of a Fatback record. New Jersey label owner Sylvia Robinson, who had a No. 3 single as an artist in 1973 with "Pillow Talk," was the first to fully realize the recorded potential of this fresh new form. After hearing a DJ at her birthday party busting rhymes over the instrumental break of a disco hit, Robinson heard something special. She hired a band to copy the backing tracks of Chic's hit "Good Times," then assembled, boy-bandlike, a trio of cats who'd never met, to rap over the music. When "Rapper's Delight" hit the streets like a ton of boomboxes, the tight rap community was confused. Nobody had ever heard of the Sugarhill Gang, and they were seen as phony interlopers. It didn't matter; the trio of Wonder Mike, Big Bank Hank and Master Gee put rap on the map.

During "Rapper's Delight"'s peak of popularity, Sugarhill was getting orders for 60,000 12-inch singles a day. Suddenly, all the rappers on the scene were putting out records. Kurtis Blow, managed by Russell Simmons, became the first superstar of rap with "The Breaks." Grandmaster Flash and the Furious Five, Afrika Bambaataa, Whodini, Funky 4 + 1, the Fat Boys and several more were pressing up vinyl as fast as they could.

Over in England, where rap was even more popular than in the States in the fall of '79, the Clash had decided to change the name of their double disc from "The Last Testament" to "London Calling." As revealed in the 30-minute "making of" DVD, which is included in the triple disc 25th anniversary of "London Calling," the original title referred to the band's intent to make the last true rock-'n'-roll record. The cover lettering, in distinctive pink and green, was a take-off on Elvis Presley's debut album. Where Elvis played the guitar on his cover, the Clash were smashing one on theirs.

Produced by madman genius Guy Stevens, who's portrayed on the DVD as a chair-thumping, ladder-throwing, wine-spilling loon, "London Calling" turned out to not be the nail in the coffin, but a call to action for other punk bands whose creative aspirations had been found in violation of "the punk police," who wanted every album to sound like the first one. The Clash dressed their host of musical ideas in horns, bouncing between roots ("Brand New Cadillac"), rock ("Lost in the Supermarket,"

"Spanish Bombs") and reggae ("Revolution Rock," "Rudie Can't Fail").

They made one more great album after "London Calling," the triple disc "Sandinista!" in 1980, then the Clash cashed in their chips with 1982's "Combat Rock." They hit the Billboard Top 10 with "Rock the Casbah," the video for which was filmed in Austin, but by the end of 1983 the two frontmen—Strummer and Jones—had split, partly because of hip-hop. Jones had gone bonkers for rap and other new dance music and wanted the Clash to play more of it. Strummer was more in a Bo Diddley/Hank Williams mood, so Jones exited and formed techno/rap/rock outfit Big Audio Dynamite.

As 1979 became the '80s, there was nothing more for punk rock to do than listen to rap. Rappers, meanwhile, were often turning to rock records for fresh beats. There was a lot of cross-pollination between New York's once-underground scenes, with CBGB grads Blondie taking rap to No. 1 with the lightweight "Rapture" and Afrika Bambaataa sampling Kraftwerk on "Planet Rock." If you reveled in being an outcast, you couldn't tick off middle-class white America more than blaring Grandmaster Flash's cut and scratch epic "Adventures on the Wheels of Steel" from your Pinto. Later came the spectacular rock/rap records of Run-DMC, which blasted hip-hop to suburbia. White kids have long embraced black culture—you can take it all the way back to Stephen Foster—and black acts have always tried to expand their white audience. But the cross-cultural exchange never flew so defiantly in the face of convention as during the advent of hip-hop.

Save a few beloved corner diners and Dolly Parton's hairstyle, almost nothing is the same as it was a quarter-century ago. Rock changed itself, and rap changed everything. White is the new black.

"Who would have ever thought that the best golfer in the world would be black and the best rapper would be white?" former NBA star Charles Barkley said a couple years ago about Tiger Woods and Eminem. Who would have ever thought that in Barkley's former profession, players would be wearing shorts that go below the knee? When you think of all the cultural scrambling that's happened since the end of the '70s, it does indeed seem like it's been 25 years.

But listen to the music that's popular today, from Kanye West and Ludacris to the Strokes and Franz Ferdinand, and 1979 could almost pass for last month.

ROBERT CHRISTGAU

In Search of Jim Crow

Why Postmodern Minstrelsy Studies Matter

In 1828 or 1829, so the story is told, in free Cincinnati or down the river in slave Louisville, or maybe in Pittsburgh (or was it Baltimore?), an obscure actor named Thomas Dartmouth "Daddy" Rice came across a crippled black stablehand doing a grotesquely gimpy dance. "Every time I turn about I jump Jim Crow," the stablehand would sing, illustrating his words with an almost literally syncopated dance ("syncope": "a partial or complete temporary suspension of respiration and circulation due to cerebral ischemia"). The effect was comical, all accounts agree; it was also rhythmically compelling or exciting, though how this effect is achieved through a discontinuity in which one half of the body is acrobatic and the other immobilized is apparently too self-evident to be addressed. Rice was so impressed that he bought the black man's clothes and made off with his song and dance. "Jump Jim Crow" became a major smash—in Gilbert Chase's words, "the first big international song hit of American popular music."

Like many European-American entertainers in the 1820s and a few going back some fifty years earlier, Rice was already appearing regularly in blackface. Not until 1843 would the Virginia Minstrels, the first (professional) (white) ("white") fiddle-banjo-tambourine-bones music group, kick off a craze that would soon accommodate interlocutors and endmen and skits and variety acts and pianos and what-have-you. In expansive mutations of fluctuating grotesquerie and brilliance, the craze would dominate American show business until the end of the nineteenth century. And after a long period of shame-faced obscurity cemented by the civil rights movement, its daunting tangle of race and class and pop culture and American music would render it a hot topic of historical debate at the end of the twentieth century. Nevertheless, Rice's strange cultural appropriation continues to stand at the headwaters of what we now call minstrelsy—its foundation myth. As a myth, the incident retains explanatory and illustrative power even though there's no way we can ascertain whether any version of it occurred.

Since the kind of reporter who would go hunting for the stablehand is rare enough in these racially sensitive times, we might expect that the sole witness on record would be Rice himself—building a colorful reputation in interviews with the press, most likely. Yet in the dozens of retellings I've checked, Rice isn't cited either; the commonest source by far—and also, remarkably, just about the earliest—is "Stephen C. Foster and Negro Minstrelsy," an article by Robert P. Nevin that appeared in the *Atlantic Monthly* in 1867, nearly forty years after the "fact," and several years as well after a by-then crippled Rice (and Foster too) had died in poverty. Even so, the appropriation could have taken place—although one would like to know more about Robert P. Nevin (whose other published writings focus on Pittsburgh, Foster's hometown)—the story was apparently an uncontroversial commonplace by the time it got to the *Atlantic*, and it has a ring, doesn't it? In fact, it's such a hell of a metaphor that one understands why few historians of minstrelsy have resisted it, and why it shows up frequently in less specialized accounts of race relations and popular music. All one would expect, especially of modern scholars attuned to the ideological baggage concealed beneath the surface of such undocumented tales, is a touch of skepticism. It's kind of amazing how rarely one gets it.

OK, it figures that old-time pop historians David Ewen and Sigmund Spaeth (for whom minstrelsy was "a black snowball which kept on rolling") would swallow the story whole. But one appreciates Gilbert Chase's simple "tradition has it," Eileen Southern's relaxed "as the story goes," and wishes recent chroniclers Christopher Small, Russell Sanjek, and Donald Clarke had exercised more caution. One knows better than to seek scholarly decorum in Carl Wittke's chatty (and useful) 1930 *Tambo and Bones*. One admires Hans Nathan's 1962 *Dan Emmett and the Rise of Early Negro Minstrelsy* for analyzing the artistic content of Rice's song and dance, and appending its supposed origin as an "it is reported" afterthought. And one is rather shocked that Robert C. Toll, whose 1974 *Blacking Up* kicked off modern minstrelsy studies; Robert Cantwell, whose 1984 *Bluegrass Breakdown* linked Bill Monroe to minstrelsy and jazz when such lineages were all but unthinkable; and Roger D. Abrahams, whose 1994 *Singing the Master* traces the minstrel-show walk-around to plantation corn-shucking festivities, buy the tale so unquestioningly.

And then there's Lawrence W. Levine, whose seminal 1977 *Black Culture and Black Consciousness* repeats the story, unfootnoted, to launch the argument that white minstrels often served as conduits from one African-American (the stablehand, "an old Louisville Negro, Jim Crow") to another (the "North Carolina Negroes shucking corn" whose virtually identical 1915 song was recorded in Newman I. White's 1928 *American Negro Folk-Songs*). One wonders what Levine would make of musicologist Charles Hamm, who in 1979 reprinted most of Nevin's *Atlantic* version in *Yesterdays: Popular Song in America*, the most thorough and thoughtful history of American pop we have. After noting the racist relish of Nevin's "colorful" style (which upon reflection evokes a minstrel stump speech), Hamm acknowledges that Rice "may have been telling the truth" before making what ought to be an obvious point: "It is equally likely that the story of the tune's origin was invented to give authenticity to a white man's portrayal of a black." Hamm believes Rice needed the help. He can discern no African elements in "Jump Jim Crow," which suggested "both an Irish folk tune and an English stage song," had small success as sheet music, and failed to enter oral tradition (unlike its counterpart, George Washington Dixon's "Zip Coon," transformed by Dan Emmett into "Turkey in the Straw"). Hamm conjectures that if Rice did indeed copy it from a black man, the black man might well have copied it earlier from a white. Conduits have a way of connecting to other conduits.

This is a reassuringly sane take on the legend. But one reason it's so sane is that it recognizes the legend's power. By quoting Nevin in all his condescending glory, Hamm implicitly recognizes why Eric Lott, whose obsessively researched 1993 *Love and Theft* kicked off postmodern minstrelsy studies, calls the *Atlantic* article, which he also quotes at length, "probably the least trustworthy and most accurate account of American minstrelsy's appropriation of black cultural practices." "According to legend—the closest we are going to get to truth in the matter" is how Lott sources the Rice story. Never mind that in her own contribution to the essay collection *Inside the Minstrel Mask*, coeditor Annemarie Bean attributes a considerably more credulous version of the story to Lott himself, because facts, likely or unlikely, have nothing on the inexorable, poetic, legendary truth. And so, completing his sentence by summing up without comment the *Atlantic* article he reproduced thirty pages before—"T. D. Rice used an old black stableman's song and dance in his first 'Jim Crow' act"—Lott launches one of his more tendentious disquisitions on, to cite jargon that has dated revealingly, "the production of the minstrel show out of gendered commodity exchange," replete with permissive definitions of bohemia, imaginative inferences of the homoerotic, century-hopping cultural generalizations, and shards of evidence that don't nearly prove what he claims they do.

Now, *Love and Theft* is a remarkable book, the most purely brilliant in minstrelsy studies. Its insistence on respecting and understanding the much-disparaged white working-class minstrel audience was long overdue. But it's too bad brilliance is the closest Lott can get to truth in the matter. I know it's only a fantasy, but let me say right here that I personally would love to know whether Rice ever actually met such a stablehand, and—if he did, which by now I doubt—exactly what cultural commodities he borrowed, arrogated, or stole.

The reason the myth remains so redolent, after all, is that it tells a story about the white-from-black "appropriation" of not just minstrelsy but all American popular music. Afro-America makes, Euro-America takes—seldom is it put so baldly, but at some level that's what many of us feel. In one line of thought, it follows that the stable-hand's "Jump Jim Crow" was intrinsically irresistible, so much so that a straight imitation made Rice a star; it follows that all that stood between the stablehand and a career in show business was the refusal of middlemen like Rice to help a black originator overcome troublesome initial audience resistance, with all projections through the next two centuries self-evident. There's an alternate possibility, however. What if Rice's "Jump Jim Crow" was a syncretic creation, sparked by components of one or more individual black performances that might even include the song itself, but incorporating as well stray elements of other songs and dances black and/or white—and also, crucially, skills, mannerisms, attitudes, and values Rice was born with, or absorbed during his long stage and idiosyncratic life experience?

This is not only what Hamm suspects, it's probably what Lott thinks too; the syncretic is as much a cultural studies trope as the trope itself. Once when discussing Rice, in fact, Lott identifies and counterposes the two models. Imitation, which he calls "theft," he links credibly to anxiety about slavery, while syncretism, "expropriation," he links dubiously to anxiety about miscegenation. Lott's reluctance to choose explicitly between them reflects not so much his scholarly modesty as his scholarly method—he'd rather explore metaphors than establish facts. But for sure the theft model dominates the other accounts I've described, and that's because Lott is surely right to align it with slavery. In whites who resist racism, the anxiety slavery provokes is rarely distinguishable anymore from guilt, in part because the rage slavery provokes in blacks is rarely masked anymore in let-bygones-be-bygones noblesse oblige. This compels whites either to share that rage or to defend themselves against it. And even more than the Confederate flag (although perhaps not the burnt cross or the KKK hood), nothing symbolizes the outrageous dehumanization of slavery as vividly for most African-Americans as "the big-lipped, bug-eyed, broad-nosed buffoons" of blackface stereotype.

The quote is from "a 26-year-old African-American who just finished reading Ted Gioia's" 2000 *New York Times* defense of Al Jolson, which was illustrated with a poster from *The Jazz Singer*. Fumed another letter writer: "Does it matter to me that [Jolson] opted for blackface to enhance the theatrical qualities of his performance and not to degrade blacks? No. What matters to me as an African-American woman is how it makes African-American people feel." Both voice an indignation that dates, in print, to Frederick Douglass, who in 1848, Lott reminds us early on, branded blackface minstrels "the filthy scum of white society, who have stolen from us a complexion denied to them by nature." For uplifters of the race like Douglass, minstrelsy's burnt cork has always seemed nothing less than a theft of identity all too precisely analagous to slavery's theft of freedom. So ever since black pride became a formula for self-actualization in the 1960s, ex-minstrel W. C. Handy's assertion that minstrelsy produced black show business has been swept under the rug. The pleasure much of the Negro audience once took, to choose the obvious example, in *Amos 'n' Andy*—in 1930, for instance, Duke Ellington's orchestra played its theme song at a Chicago Defender parade—is recalled as a tragic anomaly of benighted times, when it's acknowledged at all.

In this context, the slavery model of minstrel appropriation obviously has an insuperable advantage among African-Americans. Even when they strain to be fair, as Mel Watkins does in *On the Real Side: A History of African American Comedy*, black critics and historians are so appalled by blackface that they find it hard to work up any respect or sympathy for the white men who exploited it. The sole exception I'm aware of is Wesley Brown's 1994 novel *Darktown Strutters*, which begins with a fictionalization of the Jim Crow legend. Brown's protagonist is Jim Too, the adopted son of the crippled stablehand Jim Crow. Jim Too remakes himself as a professional dancer who also calls himself Jim Crow, but he performs without makeup, initially in Daddy Rice's troupe. Renowned and sometimes imperiled for his refusal to don the blackface that is the coin of American entertainment, he pursues a nineteenth-century African-American picaresque that makes no pretense of chronological or historical precision. Brown depicts Rice as a tortured grotesque and compulsive performer, incapable of living inside his own skin, yet "several cuts above most men I've known who do a lotta damage tryin too hard to be white."

The quote is from another white blackface artist in the historical record, dancer Jack Diamond, in Brown's story a staunch antiracist who's literally cut off at the waist at the Battle of Chancellorsville (I think—typically, Brown muddles the year). His name is found pinned to the pants that clothe his known remains, an image that soon feeds "the legend of the greatest jig dancer ever to heist his legs! And every time Jim heard another version of the story, the loss of Jack Diamond didn't weigh on him so heavily." When Afro-America makes and Euro-America takes, Brown wants us to know, sympathy is a luxury for any black person set on getting some back.

> *The story I propose here veers awry from the usual accounts of the origin of Jim Crow. That usual story, reiterated from the earliest middle-class articles on working-class performance right up through the latest scholarly accounts of minstrelsy, has it that Rice nicked "Jump Jim Crow" from a real man, usually specified as a crippled black hostler named Jim Crow. A corollary story, equally dubious, specifies a source in an individual named Cuff, who it is supposed wrestled luggage along the Pittsburgh levee.*

> *These stories are false in fact and spirit. There was no such hostler, no such baggage man. What's more, the way these stories tell it is simply not the way cultural gestures come into being.*
>
> —W. T. LHAMON JR., *RAISING CAIN*

So much for legend being the closest we are going to get to truth in the matter, at least as far as W. T. Lhamon Jr. is concerned. Lhamon is the author of two of the four major pieces of minstrelsy scholarship to follow *Love and Theft*, all almost as obsessive as Lott about secondary sources and, in the standard history-versus-theory pattern, rather more obsessive about primary sources. William J. Mahar's *Behind the Burnt Cork Mask: Early Blackface Minstrelsy and Antebellum American Popular Culture* (1999) enlists a profusion of playbills, plays, and songs to bolster a solid if flat-footed argument that minstrelsy is better understood as birthplace of showbiz than engine of racism. Dale Cockrell's *Demons of Disorder: Early Blackface Minstrels and Their World* (1997) mines court records and newspapers to connect minstrelsy to the carnivalesque class hostility of charivari and callithumpianism. Lhamon's new *Jump Jim Crow: Lost Plays, Lyrics, and Street Prose of the First Atlantic Popular Culture* is a monumental labor of textual reconstruction matched by a long and extraordinary introduction. His earlier entry, *Raising Cain: Blackface Performance From Jim Crow to Hip Hop* (1998), is more fanciful and theory-happy. Lhamon centers its well-documented vision of New York's Catherine Street Market as mixed-race cultural exchange on an 1820 folk drawing depicting three black performers "Dancing for Eels," and somewhat shakily credits George Christy with staging the first true minstrel show in Buffalo in 1842, well before the Manhattan debut of Dan Emmett's Virginia Minstrels cited by everyone else. *Raising Cain* also revealed the existence of a pamphlet called *The Life of Jim Crow* that's reprinted in *Jump Jim Crow*. Rice probably didn't write it, but he sold it at shows. It makes no mention of hostlers or baggage men.

Scornful of speculation, the text-based Mahar is one of the few historians of minstrelsy to ignore the Jim Crow legend.

Cockrell assumes the legend is true because no one bothered to deny it at the time, although he wishes he could prove the stable-hand was actually a performer at one of the black festivals he's studied. He finds its "outlines" in an 1837 Rice profile by *New York Herald* editor James Gordon Bennett, convincingly dates the song itself to 1830 rather than 1828, and refutes the truism that it was an instant hit.

Like Cockrell, Lhamon means to begin where Lott leaves off by celebrating rather than just respecting minstrelsy's audience—the counter-nobility Lhamon, following Thomas Pynchon, dubs "the mobility." But the two scholars have different agendas, and these correspond to their distinct versions of the legend. In an autobiographical epilogue, Cockrell identifies himself as a white working-class Southerner who resents Northerners' assumptions about his racism; Lhamon is cagier about personal details, putting his cultural capital on the table with stray references to Eliot, Wittgenstein, Ginsberg, Dylan, etc. Cockrell the good old boy takes for granted the kind of "borrowing" the Jim Crow legend is about and doesn't think that ends the story, citing as proof Southern musicians from Jimmie Rodgers to the Everly Brothers and "on and on, up to many of the current crop of stars." Lhamon the postmodernist emphasizes how the legend served the ideological needs of those positioned to construct and promulgate it—rival actors jealous of the popularity of this cheap craze, and privileged pundits fearful of the cross-racial class solidarity that Lhamon demonstrates coexisted with white racism, especially before the minstrel show proper.

As noted, the minstrel show proper, whether in the form of Dan Emmett's Virginia Minstrels or George Christy's much longer-lived troupe, begins in 1843, perhaps 1842. That's also the starting point for Mahar, who defines his subject as antebellum minstrelsy. In contrast, both Lhamon and Cockrell focus on the pre–1843 period; both, in fact, devote considerable attention to pre–1828 intimations. The first section of Lhamon's book teases out the 1820 drawing, while Cockrell outlines the history of "Lord of Misrule festivities." These included mumming plays,

Morris dancing, slave Christmases, West Indian John Canoe celebrations, the black elections that were quickly banned in eighteenth-century New England, Pinkster days, the German belsnickel wassails imported to Mobile by a Pennsylvania Dutch cotton broker, and callithumpian bands—soot-faced working-class youths who would roam the streets of Philadelphia, New York, and Boston around New Year's, banging drums and anything else that would make a noise until they were bought off with food and drink.

Cockrell downplays the racial significance of preminstrel blackface. Well before Rabelais, he tells us, black makeup was a way of announcing disguise and signifying Otherness, and it retained those meanings even when its overt content became racial, which onstage has been dated to 1769. He seeks out black Lord of Misrule action, and finds evidence of its influence on whites (and vice versa). But with the separate-but-equal exception of the New Orleans carnival, the actors in (as opposed to spectators at) black festivals were all black, while charivari and such excluded blacks—the belsnickels were all white, as were the callithumpians, who picked fights with black freemen as well as the ruling-class whites they were out to harass. In contrast, the Manhattan of early minstrelsy (and early Jacksonian democracy) was a hotbed of miscegenation. According to health records Lhamon unearths, the Five Points environs of Catherine Street Market were 25 percent black, with intermarriage common, and many other blacks visited the market as workers, servants, slaves, vendors, and/or, in a few cases, entertainers; Cockrell quotes heartrending court records in which cross-racial couples of the lower classes were separated by the state's Amalgamation Law.

Lhamon also connects Manhattan to George Christy's Buffalo via the Erie Canal, in whose construction he discerns a "mudsill mutuality" of black and white workers—slave, indentured, contracted, or just deeply oppressed—who constitute a key element of the lumpenproletariat Marx would conceive so contemptuously in *The 18th Brumaire*, long after the rationalization of blackface on the burgeoning minstrel circuit was getting this ruffian ragtag under control. What did Jim Crow's syncope signify? Among other things, Lhamon says, stoop labor—not the upright autonomy of Sean Wilentz's artisans, but the forced contortions of Lionel Wyld's "hoggees": "The whole stooped posture of the hoggee, permanently bent by the shovel and the barrow, and still evident in laborers today, is caught in Jim Crow's gimp."

We can't know how deeply romanticism and wishful projection distort Lhamon's and Cockrell's histories any more than we can know who really wrote "Jump Jim Crow." Cockrell himself is careful to stress the coexistence of integration and racism. Mahar, who shares the middle-class positivism associated with the Institute of Popular Culture Studies at Bowling Green (he notes with a straight face the lack of "gentlemanly refinement or common decency" in minstrel scripts) but whose main agenda is downplaying minstrelsy's racism, assumes its patrons disliked blacks and the rich "equally" and is more troubled by their offenses against women. This is wrongheaded. Nonetheless, when Lhamon observes that the "racism and vulgarity" of wealthier whites was even more pernicious, "if only because these people had far greater power to elaborate their inclinations," his argument resonates. Which racism does more harm today, after all? The working-class racism of exacerbated competition for limited resources—a competition that according to *Raising Cain* grows directly out of the bourgeois response to early minstrelsy's cross-racial threat? Or is the big hurt the ruling-class racism that still denies so many African-Americans jobs, education, housing, health care, and anything else they need?

Both Lhamon and Cockrell, moreover, take their celebration of minstrelsy's white audience a step further—they extend it to minstrelsy's white artists. Nathan's Dan Emmett book excepted, earlier minstrelsy studies can lull the most alert reader into the retrograde condescension of classic mass culture theory, in which individual producers are assumed to be hacks, schemers, cogs in a machine—and which traces back to the same class-bound notions of respectability discernible in Douglass's talented-tenth talk of "the filthy scum of white society." Lott is especially prone to this fallacy, which dovetails with cultural studies' emphasis on the social, and consequent reluctance to valorize the art hero. So much else is at stake that it's easy to forget that every minstrel song and skit was created by men whose need for display and self-expression drew them to the theatre, which isn't many people's idea of a rational career choice. Not only does Lhamon's work on Rice's plays counteract such lazy thinking—so does Cockrell's long biographical sketch of George Washington Dixon. Both make a special point of the artists' creative personal connection to the new urban culture of rootless, single young men who have been a prime pop market ever since.

The Dixon Cockrell describes was "one of the most complex, eccentric, and enigmatic men ever to have crossed the American musical stage": a skilled singer and proven songwriter, a scandal-sheet proprietor who was in jail occasionally and in court often, a hypnotist and clairvoyant and distance walker, a sometime proponent of labor abolitionism who wasn't above using music "to remold himself into an idol of the white middle class." Before he last performed in early 1843, just when the Virginia Minstrels were creating their sensation, his Ethiopian delineations had inspired many, most prominently Rice himself. In *Raising Cain*, Lhamon asserts the enduring literary value of Rice's raucous lumpen burlesques, particularly *Bone Squash Diavolo*, which the ship rigger's son who jumped Jim Crow first mounted in 1835. *Jump Jim Crow* pursues the argument by exhuming prompt manuscripts of nine plays written by or for Rice (four of each, with a ninth in doubt). Rice was obviously no Melville or Dickinson, no Whitman or Twain, no Douglass, and Lhamon avoids grand claims. But *Jump Jim Crow* opens the possibility that a blackface minstrel may yet be remembered as the most original nineteenth-century playwright in a nation whose first major dramatist was Eugene O'Neill. That would be a good joke.

Tickled though the pop advocate in me is by any transformation of hack into auteur, this one weakens a pet theory of mine. So do Mahar's dogged readings of the printed record, which establish that both cornball comedy and skirmishes in an undeclared class war are as endemic to minstrel wordplay as racist stereotypes. The theory is that logocentrism does the story of minstrelsy even less justice than it does most history—that we must somehow make the imaginative leap from the published scripts and songs to performed music, dance, and slapstick, but especially music, which constituted two-thirds of most playbills. Because African-derived usages are barely hinted by notation, minstrel music is even further beyond our ken than the rest of pre-gramophone pop. And few historians of minstrelsy are inclined to help much—Toll, Lott, Cockrell, and Lhamon are wordmen all, explicators of culture and ideology without much to say about how minstrel music altered the surrounding soundscape.

A welcome corrective is David Wondrich's groundbreaking new *Stomp and Swerve: American Music Gets Hot 1843–1924*, which puts minstrelsy first in an argument that the special heat of U.S. music (as opposed in particular to the Afro-Latin musics further south) derives from its fusion of Celtic stomp and African swerve—a perfect account of "Jump Jim Crow." After the appropriate apologies, however, Wondrich relies on Nathan for descriptive detail. The dance focus of *Raising Cain* adds something new, and in *Jump Jim Crow* Lhamon unveils a revealing Irish description of Rice's hit: "The song from which he derives his name and celebrity is paltry and vulgar—the air brief and pretty; but it has a feature that belongs to few songs—it is mostly made up of dancing. Half of each verse is chorus, and then all the chorus motion—so that it is of compound and really complex character." Lott's abstruse discussion of European versus African canons of repetition also bears pondering. In minstrel songs, he says, poetic refrain meets catch-phrase beat, ego reinforcement meets ego loss, *plaisir* meets *jouissance*, and then everyone changes partners, so complexly that even the talent and vision of individual creators may inflect how particular interactions play out and what they mean.

There's more meat in Mahar, who teaches music at Penn State–Harrisburg. Mahar interlards many useful points through his lengthy demonstrations that—gloriosky!—sexist stereotypes pervaded a theatrical form directed at young, unmarried, working-class urban males. Although most of these were known or inferred—and despite Mahar's deep reluctance to attribute distinction to Africa's rhythmic heritage or, for that matter, chattel slavery's economic one—it's still good to have them substantiated. He rides the sheet music hard, never once addressing the great unnotatables grain and groove and barely mentioning tempo. But he is aware of the "vocal inflections or gestures" sheet music misses. In explicit contradistinction to Charles Hamm, he believes (correctly, the evidence suggests) that certain minstrels—he names Joel Sweeney, Dan Emmett, and Cool White—learned a lot from black musicians, distinguishing sharply between Emmett's "limited melodic compass, modal pitch structure when performed with the banjo-fiddle instrumentation, and frequent interruption of the vocal line by instrumental breaks" and the ornately quasi-classical British product of the time. And he points out that the structure in which a single singer was accompanied by a single instrumentalist whose brief interludes accompanied dancing was "unique to blackface entertainment and the slave behavior on which it may have been based." Indeed, scandalized tales of young whites dancing to such slave behavior go back to the 1690s.

Nevertheless, our most searching investigation of minstrel music remains a few late–1970s and early–1980s articles by banjo-playing ethnomusicologist Robert B. Winans, the most important of which, "Early Minstrel-Show Music, 1843–1852," is collected in *Inside the Minstrel Mask*. To my knowledge, Winans was first to suggest the debt owed minstrelsy by white-identified styles such as blue-grass and its predecessors. But Winans resists equating minstrel music with the old-timey string bands recorded in the 1920s. For one thing, he points out, the instruments were different. The drumlike minstrel tambourine made a much louder and deeper sound than the flapjack-sized versions we know today, and the bones were far less delicate than the castanets that are their closest modern equivalent. Crucially, the banjo was bigger and deeper too, and not yet played in the chordal, "classical" style developed to accommodate the rise of the guitar in the late nineteenth century. Instead it was "frailed," struck rather than plucked, with a rhythmic emphasis that can be traced back to Africa and forward to Appalachia, where Winans believes the new beat was transported (along with many pop songs) by both traveling minstrel shows and prodigal sons who brought their city lore on home (to which Robert Cantwell would add local blacks, since no part of the South was totally white). Like Mahar, Winans—who has criticized Lott's habit of extrapolating theory from isolated songs of minimal currency in actually performed minstrelsy—cares about what songs were popular. Surviving programs reveal that at the dawn of minstrelsy proper, between 1843 and 1847, comic songs greatly predominated, only to recede between 1848 and 1852. Instead, the standard-issue heart-tuggers of nineteenth-century pop reassert themselves, with operatic parody accounting for much of the new comic material and nonsense songs like "Old Dan Tucker" and the passé "Jump Jim Crow" a vanishing fad.

Imagine an America in which stage singing was accompanied, if at all, by piano (the English-born songwriter Henry Russell), chamber trio (the protest-singing, abolitionist Hutchinson Family, a favorite blackface butt), or small opera orchestra (the run of matinee idols). Tempos and sonics suit a restless but slow-moving world in which machines are rarely heard. In the 1830s there appear performers such as Rice and Dixon, Joel Sweeney and Dan Emmett—sometimes solo, sometimes along with or in front of traditional orchestras. Cutting impolite lyrics with fancy steps, showing off on the fiddle or banjo, all are perceived as a welcome affront to the prevailing gentility by an emergent audience of rowdy young men with a few coins to throw away. But they don't break out until Emmett constructs a laff-a-minute show around a bunch of them, at which point they change everything. As Winans sums up: "they were new and different, earthy and 'exotic' at the same time, and comic and antisentimental." Toll's tribute to the Virginia Minstrels fleshes out this basic and too easily lost point: "Once on stage, they could not sit still for an instant. . . . Whether singing, dancing, or joking, whether in a featured role, accompanying a comrade, or just listening, their wild hollering and their bobbing, seemingly compulsive movements charged their entire performance with excitement. . . . From beginning to end, their shows provided an emotional outlet. Most of all, the performers seemed to have fun and succeeded in involving the foot-stomping, shouting, whistling audiences in the festivities."

Rhythmic and angular where the genteel competition was harmonic and mellifluous, hyperactive and uproarious in rhetoric and principle, minstrel music was only one part of the class drama postmodern minstrelsy studies can't get enough of. But it was the most momentous part, and the most honorable. The democratization of culture identified with the minstrel show would have happened sooner or later—P. T. Barnum didn't need minstrelsy, and neither did Hollywood (which did, however, make the most of it). But though minstrel music may have been inevitable too, putting it together required something like genius. "Jump Jim Crow" and the thousands of songs that followed established an African tendency in American pop that has waxed and waned and waxed some more ever since, with worldwide repercussions. It's hard to grasp this music's reality, as in Winans's underwhelming attempt to re-create it on an album called *The Early Minstrel Show*—the ensemble precision recalls the neat simulacra of jazz repertory, and you can hear the singers wince whenever they pronounce the word "nigger." But for all we can really know, Winans's band of ethnomusicologists on a spree may have every inflection just right. It's impossible to be sure from this side of the divide that minstrel music opened up—impossible to adjust our ears back to before blue notes, gospel melismas, ragtime, bebop, railroad trains, gramophone records, saxophones, electric guitars, Chick Webb, James Brown, punk, hiphop, the sandpaper musicality of uncounted rough baritones, and the omnipresence of more noise than can be comprehended by a Monday morning or a Saturday night.

What we can know is this: the rise of minstrelsy in the 1840s (or maybe, following Lhamon, we should say the 1830s and 1840s, privileging neither) constituted a cultural upheaval remarkably similar to the rise of rock and roll in the 1950s. Right—minstrel music was only a part of the minstrel show, which proved the foundation of the entire American entertainment industry. Right—rock and roll was only one in a series of modern musical mongrelizations, from coon song to jazz age to swing era. Nevertheless, both were benchmarks. Minstrelsy transformed blackface from a theatrical to a musical trope. It established that in a Euro-America obsessed with African retentions (the violence of the blood, the puissance of the penis, the docility of the grin), music was the star attraction, especially for the young riffraff who gave American cities their bustle. Like minstrelsy, rock and roll posed not just a racial danger, but a class danger. Although it arted itself up soon enough, a good thing as often as a bad one, it delivered pop music from status anxieties and polite facades. It made a role model of the unkempt rebel. And by finding simple tunes in the three-chord storehouse of folk modality, it cleared a space for unencumbered beat. Got it? Now ask yourself how much of the rock and roll description can be applied to minstrelsy and vice versa. Most of each for sure.

This is one reason minstrelsy's various historicizations are fascinating, and amusing, for anyone who has read many histories of rock and roll. The patterning is so similar, with specifics that go well beyond cultural reminiscence's usual golden-ageism. In both we find parallel visions of unspoiled, unpretentious white youth transcending racism in simple musical expressions soon bedizened by crass impresarios and underassistant promo men. Rock and roll has generated many golden ages—the halcyon sixties, punk in its CBGB and/or Sex Pistols clothes, and "real hiphop," to name just three. But absent romanticizations of sweet Stax music, only its original fifties version has the proper cross-racial charge, which always seems to fade. Nor is this, initially, a scholarly construction: Nick Tosches's 2001 biography of twentieth-century minstrel Emmett Miller, *Where Dead Voices*

Gather, unearths the wondrous 1854 headline "Obituary, Not Eulogistic: Negro Minstrelsy Is Dead" and tells how in 1858 George Christy's *Ethiopian Joke Book, No. 3* "bemoan[ed] the departures from genuine negrisimilitude that had begun to degrade minstrelsy." By 1930, when Duke published *Tambo and Bones*, Carl Wittke's regrets over the increasing paucity of "genuine Negro characterizations" were standard among the few who still gave thought to minstrelsy—which Tosches shows survived as a residual entertainment, especially in the South, well past its presumed death at the turn of the century and in fact past World War II.

Where Dead Voices Gather is typical Tosches cup-half-empty: killer prose and genius archive-digging stunk up with dull contempt for academics more soulful than he is and the racial philosophy of Joe Colombo. But give it credit for insisting, early and often, that no concept is as corrupt as purity: "Blackface, white face, false face. 'Originality is but high-born stealth.' These may be the only words written by Edward Dahlberg that are worth remembering; and who knows where he got them." Originality, purity, their toney cousin authenticity—as rhetorical tools, all are made to order for a conservative agenda. If, as Charles Hamm says, the Jim Crow legend meant "to give authenticity to a white man's portrayal of a black," was the intention to fend off objections from Afro-American intellectuals? Of course not. As Lhamon argues, powerful Americans feared the race-defying underclass impulses minstrelsy's aesthetic made manifest. Whether those impulses were genuinely African-American matters less than that they scared gatekeepers, who often responded with the belittling claim, a shrewd fusion of cooptation and condemnation, that they were inauthentic—and still do, sometimes.

In *Jump Jim Crow*, Lhamon shows how supposedly sympathetic middle-class observers attacked Rice's credibility with invidious comparisons—to "the veritable James" discovered by actress-diarist Fanny Kemble among the slaves on her husband's

Georgia sea islands plantation, or to black New Orleans songster and acknowledged Rice-influenced Old Corn Meal. Inevitably, incongruent details were ignored. How veritable did Kemble find her black servants when she censured their "transparent plagiarism" of "Scotch or Irish airs"? Was Old Corn Meal still the real thing when he performed Rice's "Sich a Gittin' Up Stairs"? Certainly some impresario could have made a few bucks putting Old Corn Meal on tour, as soon happened with freeborn black tap pioneer William Henry "Juba" Lane, the toast of London in the 1840s, who died there broke before he reached thirty. As with millions of other racist injustices, that it didn't happen is a disgrace—it should have happened a hundred times over. But it's also racist to assume that, if it had happened a hundred times over, the flood of pure African-American art would have been the undoing of Daddy Rice and all his kind. Somewhere in that cross-racial nexus lurked a uniquely American sensibility whose decisive attraction was that it was no respecter of propriety. And though it proved far less dangerous than the powers feared, they fear it still.

It's misguided to overload this sensibility with political meaning, or to declare it irrelevant after that potential plays itself out. Inconsequentiality was one of its attractions. The signal term is an elusive one: "fun," which starts picking up O.E.D. citations just as minstrelsy gets going in the 1830s. The Christy Minstrels invited audiences "to see the fun, to hear the songs, and help to right the 'niggers' wrongs"; circus press agent Charles H. Day published an 1874 history of minstrelsy called *Fun in Black*. By Emmett Miller's time, the trades and dailies were using "funmakers" and "the fun contingent" as ready synonyms for blackface performers. Struck by "the regularity with which observers resorted to the word 'fun' to describe their enjoyment of blacks and of blackface," Lott calls a whole chapter "'Genuine Negro Fun'"—and turns out to care at least as much about the "Fun" part, which is hard to parse, as the "Genuine Negro" part, too patent to merit unpacking.

To his credit, Lott emphasizes that what he takes for minstrelsy's attempts to "tame the 'black' threat" always risk leaving something untoward in the woodpile. But it should go without saying that he executes his analysis from on high. All this fun, he is certain, has the function of mitigating a "roiling jumble of need, guilt, and disgust." The less said the better about his Freudian readings of blackface usage—although I'm certain he overdoes them, I'm probably too skeptical. Let me merely cite his tendency to assume the worst about the minstrel audience of the 1840s, when he believes working-class consciousness, disemboldened by the Panic of 1837, was fleeing politics at every turn and with no exception. Of more moment is his disapproval of the Christy-style minstrel show's presumably parallel flight into spectacle from narrative, meaning plays like Rice's. And crucial is his search for the meaning of fun in jokes, costumes, and business, ignoring the music that was foregrounded during precisely the same period. We've been here before, but let's ratchet up our objections by emphasizing that—where Rice, for instance, worked solo-with-backup—the Virginia Minstrels and their progeny were *bands*. Rock and rollers know the difference, which is usually fun in a way that barely suggests race or class while saying much that's otherwise inexpressible about human interaction.

And now for Freud. At a crucial juncture, Lott cites the patriarch himself, unmasking fun as "lost moments of childish pleasure evoked by the antics of children, or of 'inferior' people who resemble them": "constant repetition," "supreme disorderly conduct," "oversized clothes," "performative irruption," "the gorging and mucus-mongering of early life." Perhaps Lott would be less discomfited by this structure of feeling if he tried harder to distinguish between children and infants, but either way it can be explicated sans Freud. The idealization of childhood is a well-known tenet of romanticism and hence our era, throughout which it has been disparaged to no avail by pundits and cynics of every stripe. And admittedly, returning to childhood is a lousy way to pass laws or get the laundry done, a journey that's always doomed in the end. But in a system where the same can be said of many other things worth doing in themselves, an idealized youth is a hell of a good place for low-level ungovernables with dirty drawers to spend Saturday night, a site of worldly transcendence in which egoisms needn't always get in the way of other egoisms. It's a satisfaction, a recourse, damn right an escape—a feat of imagination. We should be grateful that it no longer involves big-lipped buffoons with their feets too big. But we should be proud that it's been a special destination of American popular music since more or less the time of "Jump Jim Crow."

Jump Jim Crow's collected narratives are unlikely to leave Rice our first important playwright. Literary arbiters are literary arbiters, after all, and anyway, the plays aren't good enough. Not only are several by English actors with ties to drawing-room farce who'd rather Jim were a prince from the Congo than a ne'er-do-well from the Five Points, but only two of Rice's much impress. The stunner is *Bone Squash*, a dizzying one-act "burletta" full of nonsense, deviltry, and love sweet love that ends with the Jim figure ascending heavenward in a balloon—an image of orgasm, Lhamon ventures, far more convincingly than Lott finding phallic symbols whenever he turns over a lithograph. Yet equally remarkable is Rice's burlesque of *Otello*, first mounted in 1844, perhaps as a rebuke to the mobility after the Christys bigged up his act. Lhamon relates much worth reading about Othello in pre-Civil War culture, with two of Rice's strokes crying out for special mention. First, Othello and Desdemona have a baby—not one of the high yallers blackface poked fearful fun at, but a chiaroscuro pied piper in potentia, his face half black and half white. Before too long, you just know, he'll be strumming on the old banjo. Second, Othello isn't reassuringly tragic. He doesn't die. At the end of the play he and his issue are triumphantly alive.

But rather than exit on that encouraging note, let me cite another idea Lhamon lets slip. Unlike the transparently racist construction Sambo, Lhamon argues proudly, Jim Crow is not docile: "his lyrics show him fighting 'white dandies,' Jersey blacks, and Philadelphia Sambos." Lhamon goes on: "This transgressive power of Jim Crow is what the political regime of Jim Crow laws in the South projected on all African Americans, of every class, and then used to contain them as a category after the North's betrayal of Reconstruction."

What he doesn't add is this: To hell with art. To hell with Saturday night. Why shouldn't African-Americans hate Jim Crow?

This is a damning indictment. If "Jump Jim Crow" lay behind the machinery of state-mandated racial segregation, what can mitigate that? But if segregation was inevitable anyway, then perhaps its naming only represents a setback for a people's culture we must struggle to reclaim. So permit me one final story.

Abraham Lincoln loved a joke, loved music, and loved minstrel music. He was an instant fan of the infernally catchy "Dixie," composed by Dan Emmett in 1859—though it has also been attributed to the black Snowden family, sometime professional musicians from Ohio who shared music with Emmett—and soon expropriated as the Confederate anthem. Right after Appomattox, Lincoln asked an attendant band to strike up "Dixie"—"one of the best tunes I ever heard." It was our "lawful property" now, he joshed. Would it had been that simple.

By then Lincoln's musical tastes had gotten him in trouble. Two weeks after the battle of Antietam—23,000 dead and wounded on September 17, 1862, the bloodiest day in American history—Lincoln met nearby with General George McClellan, soon to be relieved of his command for excessive caution. In the president's party was his former law partner Ward Lamon, who served as a bodyguard and wielded a mean hand on the banjo. Dispirited by the shadow of death and his distrust of McClellan, Lincoln asked Lamon for a lost weeper by one W. Willing called "Twenty Years Ago," but that just made him bluer. So Lamon tried the cheerful minstrel standard "Picayune Butler," named for a black New Orleans colleague of Old Corn Meal. When Lincoln remained despondent, Lamon gave up. At no point did McClellan object.

Within months the story was out in the opposition press. Lincoln, always archly characterized as a clown or jester, had insulted the dead of Antietam "before the corpses had been buried" by calling for "a negro melody"—identified first as "Jim Along Josey," then "Picayune Butler," and eventually, what else, "Jump Jim Crow." During the 1864 campaign, with McClellan his opponent, the lies and vilification intensified. Always at issue was the crass, low, common, unserious vulgarity that disqualified this smutmonger turned abolitionist from pursuing the peace as sixteenth magistrate of the United States. Always the proof was not just his insensitive choice of occasion, but his attraction to what was always called a "negro" song—not "nigger," thank you very much, but never "minstrel" either. This at a time when the blackface brethren of the Northern stage were pumping McClellan for all they were worth, which by then, Lhamon and the others have it right, wasn't much—not culturally, anyway.

We may feel that Lincoln was also too cautious—that he should have freed the slaves sooner, that as with almost every white American of the nineteenth century, his racial attitudes were lamentable. We may also feel that minstrel music did the freed slaves more harm than good. But this incident suggests a kinder interpretation. Full-bore racists of the gatekeeping classes didn't care how authentic "Picayune Butler" was. It was close enough to colored to alarm them just because it evoked a world in which bastard spawn like Abraham Lincoln could get past the gatekeepers. Not only that, some voters thought such songs fun, and fun worth pursuing. That alarmed them too. Daddy Rice and Dan Emmett must have been doing something right.

DAVE EGGERS

And Now, a Less Informed Opinion

They were earnest Scotsmen who sang of mountains and famine and bloody battles. They wore plaid flannel shirts. They danced a jig. They were Big Country, and they are wrongly forgotten.

There are certain inevitabilities in life, all of which we have known, consciously or otherwise, since we were very young. One is that all earthly existence will one day perish in an apocalypse of our own making. Another: We can expect that until that time, food will be made ever more good-tasting and aerodynamic. Lastly, we have all been certain, no matter how hard we tried to deny it, that this column would one day be devoted to the music of Big Country. That one day is this day, which is now. Thursday.

I discovered Big Country through one of the non-MTV video shows, most likely *Friday Night Videos*, which used to air on NBC in the early '80s. The "In a Big Country" clip featured the band (presumably—they were wearing helmets) riding around Scotland on ATVs, chasing some willful young lass. But I bought *The Crossing*, Big Country's 1983 debut album, as many did, not only because the sound was so distinctive—the guitars as bagpipes—but because when they sang about the largeness of the land and how it might inspire someone needing uplift, they seemed completely serious.

Stuart Adamson, the band's singer and songwriter, wrote about Scotland—not the new, semi-Americanized Scotland growing in the cities of Glasgow or Edinburgh, but the old Highlands Scotland of glacial creation and gray skies and evil English lords and William Wallace. There were songs on *The Crossing* about famine ("Harvest Home"), missionaries making their way home in the dark ("Lost Patrol"), and great bloody battles ("Fields of Fire"). All were grand, all were panoramic. Even the occasional love song ("1000 Stars") sounded as if a man and a woman were breaking up on the edge of a rocky, windswept cliff.

The album's inner sleeve was illustrated with black-and-white renderings of lighthouses, oceans, men dodging falling rocks. The band's logo included a compass. A compass! Who else, except perhaps John Denver, about whom no more shall be said, has dared to write songs about the land, about mountains and storms? With Mark Brzezicki's martial drumming and Adamson's booming voice, the album was intimate yet vast, gritty yet atmospheric, universal yet fervently nationalistic. Listening to it, you really felt—prepare for a word this magazine will regret publishing—*transported.* Even the band's videos sought to immerse you in a frigidly exotic place and time. While U2 rode horses in the snow in "New Year's Day," Big Country dressed as World War I soldiers and ran through minefields in "Fields of Fire." It was so corny it ached, but its unfettered earnestness was welcome, given the vapidity of the era.

Big Country were born in 1981, when the United Kingdom was producing some of the most ludicrous music ever devised. Synthesizers had sent thousands of actual-instrument-playing musicians onto the dole, and most successful bands traveled with a hair architect, a jeans ripper, and someone to tie scarves around the members' necks and ankles. Still, there was some good music to be found, smart, tight pop that took punk's energy and polished it, exploding the fatuousness of Boston-Journey-ELO spaceship rock, stripping things down, bringing it back to Earth. Squeeze made it, as did XTC, Elvis Costello, and the Go-Go's.

We listen to their tight, well-crafted songs and we think, "*Of course!* This is the way songs are supposed to be—they should be neat and polished and no more than three minutes long." There are no loose ends, no mistakes, and this gives us a sense, dare we say, of the order we can make of the world.

But then we hear something different. We hear something huge and loose and flawed, and when that somehow works, we switch our allegiance and we say, "No, no—*this* is it, *this* is the way it should be." Such music unravels everything we know but makes that unraveling, that fraying of all order, feel like the best idea anyone's ever had. It hits higher highs and lower lows, and by the end, you wind up somewhere very different from where you began. This is the Epic Album, achieved by bands like U2, Radiohead, and, most recently, the Walkmen (holy lord, that record is great). The difference between the tidy song/Perfect Album and the crazy song/Epic Album is the difference between driving an efficient, shiny sports car that can accelerate quickly and turn on a dime and driving an 18-wheeler at 200 miles an hour and having it take off, become airborne, and just barely miss flying into a mountain.

The Crossing was that kind of album.

So I started following pretty much everything Big Country did. I was too young (13) to go to a concert at a club—and I don't even know if they made it to Chicago—but I caught them when they gave a short TV interview, which I taped on our new Montgomery Ward VCR. Stuart Adamson sat with bassist Tony Butler, at that point the only black man I'd ever heard speak with a Scottish accent. Adamson was pasty, his hair short but gelled in a bedhead style, his eyes small, close-set, and dark. He looked and sounded like a Boy Scout, talking very solemnly about how few bands were making real music, how slick and uninspired things had become.

He and Butler were wearing plaid shirts—one red, one blue. Big Country wore a lot of plaid. This was an era when bands, like the image-conscious gangs in *The Warriors*, wore matching outfits:

The Jacksons had their space-admiral look, Dexy's Midnight Runners had their waif-in-overalls motif, and Bananarama . . . also had a waif-in-overalls motif. And though such ensembles, even then, seemed tragic, Big Country's somehow felt unplanned, as if the members all happened to show up, night after night, photo shoot after photo shoot, in plaid shirts, presumably selected from closets holding nothing else. These men were so unmistakably sincere that everything they did defied pity or suspicion.

I can't say it was all Big Country's doing, but I too started wearing a lot of flannel. That winter I walked through the snow for hours listening to *The Crossing*, jumping down ravines, looking for caves, walking on frozen lakes, letting in the cold. I would come home chilled to the bone, my feet itchy from the onset of frostbite, but I felt stoic, like I knew something about the fighting men of the harsh Scottish countryside. It was sad, yes, but this is the kind of experience-through-osmosis adolescents usually get by reading *Wuthering Heights* or *Dune*, not from listening to an *album*. How many bands could claim to have created, in ten songs, an entire troubled, inspired, rainy, sorrowful but persevering *world*?

Big Country became well known for their live shows, which were spirited, revival-like. During "Fields of Fire" they often did a sort of jig, kicking at the same time, left and right, a little bit Highlands, a little bit rock 'n' roll. I eventually found a live import of a New Year's Eve concert in Edinburgh. At the end of the show, while the drummer did a long snare buildup to "In a Big Country," Adamson spoke to the audience, out of breath. "I just want to say . . . " he said, then he seemed to lose his train of thought. "I just want to say . . . " he repeated, and trailed off again. After a long pause, he finished: "I just want to say . . . stay alive." He spoke the words very quickly, as if for whatever reason they were difficult to get out. At least that's how I remember it. Then the band kicked in.

Big Country's next two recordings, 1984's *Wonderland* EP and *Steeltown*, were every bit as good as *The Crossing*, but the quartet never had another hit in the U.S. Eventually they seemed to capitulate to what they felt the American market wanted, creating a series of shatteringly mainstream singles, as if Adamson had been possessed by Kip Winger. Or Kip Winger's less talented brother. Worse, the band traded in their denim and flannel for tapered linen pants and *Miami Vice* jackets. It was rough.

And now, while a series of '80s bands have been eulogized or even resurrected, nobody talks much about Big Country. Maybe it's because they defy classification. Those interested in the kitsch value of the era might recall Big Country for their plaid and for committing Rock Sin No. 41—having a song with their name in it—but any deeper look into their music separates them from the Kajagoogoos or Dramaramas. Big Country had an original take on the world and might have followed a path similar to U2's—their sound was just as big, and Adamson's worldview was just as idealistic. Yet before they had the chance to make the leap from curiosity to full respectability—a leap made by Beck, the Beastie Boys, and others who started their careers with a misunderstood crossover hit—they abandoned what made them distinctive. And many of their loyalists deserted them.

Stuart Adamson hanged himself in a hotel room in Hawaii in 2001, at the age of 43. He'd disappeared a few weeks earlier from his home in Tennessee, where he'd moved in 1997. He'd struggled with alcoholism for years, and an autopsy revealed that at the time of his death, he had a blood-alcohol level over 0.2. His passing made the wire services, but it wasn't big news in America. It had been, after all, 18 years since "In a Big Country." But for those who still cared—and there are dozens of websites that dissect every word he wrote and publicly spoke—Adamson's death was as affecting as anyone's, including Kurt Cobain's.

For the previous six months, I'd been in touch with the band's manager, Ian Grant, because I was planning to write something about Big Country—I didn't know what, maybe a short biography, or a tribute; I wasn't sure. Grant told me that Adamson was living in Nashville with his wife, who owned a beauty parlor, and that he was writing country music with a band called the Raphaels. At some point while we were trying to arrange a time for me to visit, news of Adamson's disappearance arrived. The official Big Country website posted pleas to fans to report any sightings. It was devastating to watch it all unfold.

Kurt Cobain's suicide wasn't entirely surprising. His head was known to be a dark and tortured place, and there were countless clues that he might someday choose an early exit. But it's harder to get your mind around things, isn't it, when someone whose vision seemed so positive and outward-focusing decides to end his life. How can a man who finished his concerts with the words "stay alive," the words spoken to throngs of young people as they looked up at him soaked in sweat and grinning, hang himself in a Hawaii hotel room?

There's no moral here. There are lessons, maybe, but they cancel each other out. Lesson: Don't forget who you are, and don't pretend to be, say, Kip Winger or a country singer from Nashville. On the other hand: Was Adamson supposed to play Scot-rock in plaid flannel all his life? Lesson: More bands should write about the land, the sky, soldiers, storms, oceans; the world is vast and rock music is uniquely poised to reflect that. Counterpoint: One false move and you've got Gordon Lightfoot's "Wreck of the Edmund Fitzgerald." Lesson: Go buy *The Crossing*. Listen to the eight-minute "Porrohman" and tell me these guys didn't know something about soul and suffering and uplift. Counterpoint: There is no counterpoint to that one. Final lesson: Support your local Epic Album makers. Let the Walkmen and Interpol and Grandaddy know they're necessary to the mix, lest they take the easy way out.

SASHA FRERE-JONES

1979

The Year Punk Died, and Was Reborn

In 1979, The Clash were experiencing some pressure. Whether they wanted it or not, punk rock had become their responsibility. In New York, the Ramones had come up with the musical idea of reducing rock to three chords, doubling the volume, and accelerating songs until they sounded like Morse code. In London, the Sex Pistols had turned disgust into an ideology and made punk a historical moment, inspiring teen-agers across England to start bands. But by March of 1979 the Ramones had become more interested in being themselves than in changing the world, the Sex Pistols had disbanded, and The Clash, feeling burned out, had fired the manager who helped put the band together, in 1976. Yet they still owed CBS a record.

The Clash were able to fit more music and faith through the keyhole of punk than anyone else. Their début album, "The Clash," was a brick in flight, fourteen songs, half of them under two minutes long. The lyrics talk about the riots the band members want to start, the American imperialism they want to stop, and England's general lack of "career opportunities." It is an act of political resistance and pure pleasure. Their second album, "Give 'Em Enough Rope," was criticized for having an allegedly American sheen, but you'd have trouble hearing that now. The music is hard and echoey, barking but sweetly melodic. Actually, no—the hierarchy is more specific than that. Someone is singing sweetly way in the back, behind the loud guitars, and there's a very loud singer in the front who sounds like he's going to die if he doesn't get to sing *right now*. The one in the back is Mick Jones, the guitarist, who wrote most of The Clash's music, and the one in the front is Joe Strummer, who wrote and sang most of the lyrics, if singing is the right word. Strummer delivered words as if there were no such things as amplification and he would have been willing to run around town singing through a tube if he had to.

Strummer's moral authority, coupled with Jones's ability to synthesize decades of rock music without seeming too clever, made people care about The Clash, personally, intensely, and totally. When the band, not yet a year old, signed with CBS in 1977, the London fanzine writer Mark Perry said, "Punk died the day The Clash signed to CBS." Perry was only taking the band as seriously as they took themselves. Strummer, especially, believed that punk should be available to all, and felt inherently hostile to authority. Paradoxically, it was the corporate paymaster CBS that eventually ran ads for The Clash with the tagline "The only band that matters." In March of 1979, everyone, including The Clash, knew that the hype might be more than hype. But how could a rock band possibly live up to those expectations?

By releasing "London Calling," sixty-five minutes of rock music that never goes wrong. Without self-importance, the music covers huge amounts of ground. The stories hang together with the weight of commandments and the serendipitous grace of a pile of empty bottles. Montgomery Clift becomes a folk hero ("The Right Profile"), the myth of Stagger Lee is resurrected for a new audience ("Wrong 'Em, Boyo"), and London burns. Nothing sounds forced or insincere, not the breezy cover of an obscure English rockabilly song ("Brand New Cadillac") or fantasies of being a Jamaican bad boy ("Revolution Rock"). Hyperbole itself cannot diminish this record. Each of us is invincible when it's playing.

Now reissued in a new boxed set, "London Calling" comes with a bonus CD of rehearsals and a DVD documentary about the making of the album and original promo clips. This generosity would have pleased Strummer, who died in 2002, but he likely would have been less thrilled that the set lists for $29.98. When the album was originally released, as a two-LP set, the band felt that their records had to be priced for punks and insisted that CBS sell it for $9.98.

The documentary and the rough rehearsal demos make the same point: The Clash worked fiendishly hard to be magical. In an on-camera interview, Strummer says, "For some reason, we weren't night-clubbing people. All I can remember is writing and rehearsing and recording. A real intensity of effort." The rehearsals are evidence that the songs on "London Calling" were almost entirely worked out before the record's producer, Guy Stevens, was even hired. The only remaining task was to record the music. How Stevens, who died of an overdose of an anti-alcohol medication two years later, helped do this is unclear; thanks to this DVD, history will remember him as the guy who threw chairs and swung ladders about while The Clash recorded.

On "London Calling," Strummer remakes his major points: the police are on the wrong side, wage labor will crush your soul, and sometimes people need to destroy property to be heard. His sense of righteousness is enhanced by the album's sequencing, which feels Biblically logical and begins with one of the best opening songs of any record ever, the title track. The song starts cold. Two guitar chords ring on the downbeats, locked in step with the drums, marching forward with no dynamic variation. A second guitar introduces difference, coming toward us like an ambulance Dopplering into range. The bass guitar, sounding like someone's voice, heralds everybody over the hill and into the song. If you can listen to it without getting a chilly burst of immortality, there is a layer between you and the world. Joe Strummer simultaneously watches the riots and sloughs off his role as de-facto punk president: "London calling, now don't look to us / All that phony Beatlemania has bitten the dust / London calling, see we ain't got no swing / 'Cept for the ring of that truncheon thing." The chorus forms a keystone for the whole album: "A nuclear error, but I have no fear / London is drowning and I, I live by the river." The Clash are laughing at Margaret Thatcher and will be dancing long after the police have come and gone.

And what can you call this generous mountain of music, this sound that levitates around its own grievances like a plane on fire? Is it chopped-up rock? Very loud reggae? Some kind of devotional punk? The sensation of hearing several kinds of music at once runs through the album. Reggae is a force that permeates much of it, both as a source of topical songwriting and as a sound, but nothing on the album is strictly reggae. A song like the massive "Clampdown" shifts naturally through three sections: the four huge, descending chords big enough to open a season at Bayreuth; the dancing, pendulous rock of the verses; and the taunting funk of the bridge. The song fades away in a vamp that sounds like disco, so light you might get the impression the band had forgotten everything they'd just sung about: institutional racism, political brainwashing, and the creeping compromise of working life. "You start wearing the blue and brown / You're working for the clampdown / So you got someone to boss around / It makes you feel big now." The hectoring is never so simple that you don't wonder if they're directing it partly at themselves.

The album's soul might be found in "The Guns of Brixton," by the group's bassist, Paul Simonon. It's reggae thickened up and filtered by musicians who don't exactly know how to play reggae but love it completely. Their heavy hands make it something new. Simonon is a croaky and untrained singer, and this only enhances his convictions: "When they kick at your front door / How you gonna come? / With your hands on your head / Or on the trigger of your gun?" Threatening your rivals and writing scatological lyrics is one way to be "controversial." Staring down the riot police is another.

If Strummer's instincts were not his alone, then somewhere right now a kid is throwing a fancy, overpriced package of twenty-five-year-old material across the room and pledging to reinvent punk rock once and for all, doubting her heroes while carrying their astonishing music in her whole body.

ROBERT HILBURN

Rock's Enigmatic Poet Opens a Long-Private Door

Amsterdam—"No, no, no," Bob Dylan says sharply when asked if aspiring songwriters should learn their craft by studying his albums, which is precisely what thousands have done for decades.

"It's only natural to pattern yourself after someone," he says, opening a door on a subject that has long been off-limits to reporters: his songwriting process. "If I wanted to be a painter, I might think about trying to be like Van Gogh, or if I was an actor, act like Laurence Olivier. If I was an architect, there's Frank Gehry.

"But you can't just copy somebody. If you like someone's work, the important thing is to be exposed to everything that person has been exposed to. Anyone who wants to be a songwriter should listen to as much folk music as they can, study the form and structure of stuff that has been around for 100 years. I go back to Stephen Foster."

For four decades, Dylan has been a grand American paradox: an artist who revolutionized popular songwriting with his nakedly personal yet challenging work but who keeps us at such distance from his personal life—and his creative technique—that he didn't have to look far for the title of his recent movie: "Masked and Anonymous."

Although fans and biographers might read his hundreds of songs as a chronicle of one man's love and loss, celebration and outrage, he doesn't revisit the stories behind the songs, per se, when he talks about his art this evening. What's more comfortable, and perhaps more interesting to him, is the way craft lets him turn life, ideas, observations and strings of poetic images into songs.

As he sits in the quiet of a grand hotel overlooking one of the city's picturesque canals, he paints a very different picture of his evolution as a songwriter than you might expect of an artist who seemed to arrive on the pop scene in the '60s with his vision and skills fully intact. Dylan's lyrics to "Blowin' in the Wind" were printed in *Broadside*, the folk music magazine, in May 1962, the month he turned 21.

The story he tells is one of trial and error, false starts and hard work—a young man in a remote stretch of Minnesota finding such freedom in the music of folk songwriter Woody Guthrie that he felt he could spend his life just singing Guthrie songs—until he discovered his true calling through a simple twist of fate.

Dylan has often said that he never set out to change pop songwriting or society, but it's clear he was filled with the high purpose of living up to the ideals he saw in Guthrie's work. Unlike rock stars before him, his chief goal wasn't just making the charts.

"I always admired true artists who were dedicated, so I learned from them," Dylan says, rocking slowly in the hotel room chair. "Popular culture usually comes to an end very quickly. It gets thrown into the grave. I wanted to do something that stood alongside Rembrandt's paintings."

Even after all these years, his eyes still light up at the mention of Guthrie, the "Dust Bowl" poet, whose best songs, such as "This Land Is Your land," spoke so eloquently about the gulf Guthrie saw between America's ideals and its practices.

"To me, Woody Guthrie was the be-all and end-all," says Dylan, 62, his curly hair still framing his head majestically as it did on album covers four decades ago. "Woody's songs were about everything at the same time. They were about rich and poor, black and white, the highs and lows of life, the contradictions between what they were teaching in school and what was really happening. He was saying everything in his songs that I felt but didn't know how to.

"It wasn't only the songs, though. It was his voice—it was like a stiletto—and his diction. I had never heard anybody sing like that. His guitar strumming was more intricate than it sounded. All I knew was I wanted to learn his songs."

Dylan played so much Guthrie during his early club and coffeehouse days that he was dubbed a Woody Guthrie "jukebox." So imagine the shock when someone told him another singer—Ramblin' Jack Elliott—was doing that too. "It's like being a doctor who has spent all these years discovering penicillin and suddenly [finding out] someone else has already done it," he recalls.

A less ambitious young man might have figured no big deal—there's plenty of room for two singers who admire Guthrie. But Dylan was too independent. "I knew I had something that Jack didn't have," he says, "though it took a while before I figured out what it was."

Songwriting, he finally realized, was what could set him apart. Dylan had toyed with the idea earlier, but he felt he didn't have enough vocabulary or life experience.

Scrambling to distinguish himself on the New York club scene in 1961, though, he tried again. The first song of his own that drew attention to him was "Song to Woody," which included the lines, "Hey, hey, Woody Guthrie . . . I know that you know / All the things that I'm a-sayin' an' a-many times more."

Within two years, he had written and recorded songs, including "Girl of the North Country" and "A Hard Rain's A-Gonna Fall," that helped lift the heart of pop music from sheer entertainment to art.

"Songs Are the Star"

Dylan, whose work and personal life have been dissected in enough books to fill a library wall, seems to welcome the chance to talk about his craft, not his persona or history. It's as if he wants to demystify himself.

"To me, the performer is here and gone," he once said. "The songs are the star of the show, not me."

He also hates focusing on the past. "I'm always trying to stay right square in the moment. I don't want to get nostalgic or narcissistic as a writer or a person. I think successful people don't dwell in the past. I think only losers do."

Yet his sense of tradition is strong. He likes to think of himself as part of a brotherhood of writers whose roots are in the raw country, blues and folk strains of Guthrie, the Carter Family, Robert Johnson and scores of Scottish and English balladeers.

Over the course of the evening, he offers glimpses into how his ear and eye put pieces of songs together using everything from Beat poetry and the daily news to lessons picked up from contemporaries.

He is so committed to talking about his craft that he has a guitar at his side in case he wants to demonstrate a point. When his road manager knocks on the door after 90 minutes to see if everything is OK, Dylan waves him off. After three hours, he volunteers to get together again after the next night's concert.

"There are so many ways you can go at something in a song," he says. "One thing is to give life to inanimate objects. Johnny Cash is good at that. He's got the line that goes, 'A freighter said, "She's been here, but she's gone, boy, she's gone."' That's great. 'A freighter says' "She's been here."' That's high art. If you do that once in a song, you usually turn it on its head right then and there."

The process he describes is more workaday than capturing lightning in a bottle. In working on "Like a Rolling Stone," he says, "I'm not thinking about what I want to say, I'm just thinking 'Is this OK for the meter?'"

But there's an undeniable element of mystery too. "It's like a ghost is writing a song like that. It gives you the song and it goes away, it goes away. You don't know what it means. Except the ghost picked me to write the song."

Some listeners over the years have complained that Dylan's song are too ambiguous—that they seem to be simply an exercise in narcissistic wordplay. But most critics say Dylan's sometimes competing images are his greatest strength.

Few in American pop have consistently written lines as hauntingly beautiful and richly challenging as his "Just Like a Woman," a song from the mid-'60s:

Nobody feels any pain
Tonight as I stand inside
the rain
Ev'rybody knows
That Baby's got new clothes
But lately I see her ribbons and her bows
Have fallen from her curls.
She takes just like a woman, yes, she does
She makes love just like a woman, yes, she does
And she aches just like a woman
But she breaks just like
a little girl.

Dylan stares impassively at a lyric sheet for "Just Like a Woman" when it is handed to him. As is true of so many of his works, the song seems to be about many things at once.

"I'm not good at defining things," he says. "Even if I could tell you what the song was about I wouldn't. It's up to the listener to figure out what it means to him."

As he stares at the page in the quiet of the room, however, he budges a little. "This is a very broad song. A line like, 'Breaks just like a little girl' is a metaphor. It's like a lot of blues-based songs. Someone may be talking about a woman, but they're not really talking about a woman at all. You can say a lot if you use metaphors."

After another pause, he adds: "It's a city song. It's like looking at something extremely powerful, say the shadow of a church or something like that. I don't think in lateral [sic] terms as a writer. That's a fault of a lot of the old Broadway writers . . . They are so lateral. There's no circular thing, nothing to be learned from the song, nothing to inspire you. I always try to turn a song on its head. Otherwise, I figure I'm wasting the listener's time."

Discovering Folk Music

Dylan's pop sensibilities were shaped long before he made his journey east in the winter of 1960–61.

Growing up in the icy isolation of Hibbing, Minn., Dylan, who was still Robert Allen Zimmerman then, found comfort in the country, blues and early rock 'n' roll that he heard at night on a Louisiana radio station whose signal came in strong and clear. It was worlds away from the local Hibbing station, which leaned toward mainstream pop like Perry Como, Frankie Laine and Doris Day.

Dylan has respect for many of the pre-rock songwriters, citing Cole Porter, whom he describes as a "fearless" rhymer, and Porter's "Don't Fence Me In" as a favorite. But he didn't feel most of the pre-rock writers were speaking to him.

"When you listen to [Porter's] songs and the Gershwins' and Rodgers and Hammerstein, who wrote some great songs, they were writing for their generation and it just didn't feel like mine," he says. "I realized at some point that the important thing isn't just how you write songs, but your subject matter, your point of view."

The music that did speak to him as a teenager in the '50s was rock 'n' roll—especially Elvis Presley. "When I got into rock 'n' roll, I didn't even think I had any other option or alternative," he says. "It showed me where my future was, just like some people know they are going to be doctors or lawyers or shortstop for the New York Yankees."

He became a student of what he heard.

"Chuck Berry wrote amazing songs that spun words together in a remarkably complex way," he says. "Buddy Holly's songs were much more simplified, but what I got out of Buddy was that you can take influences from anywhere. Like his 'That'll Be the Day.' I read somewhere that it was a line he heard in a movie, and I started realizing you can take things from everyday life that you hear people say.

"That I still find true. You can go anywhere in daily life and have your ears open and hear something, either something someone says to you or something you hear across the room. If it has resonance, you can use it in a song."

After rock took on a blander tone in the late '50s, Dylan looked for new inspiration. He began listening to the Kingston Trio, who helped popularize folk music with polished versions of "Tom Dooley" and "A Worried Man." Most folk purists felt the group was more "pop" than authentic, but Dylan, new to folk, responded to the messages in the songs.

He worked his way through such other folk heroes as Odetta and Leadbelly before fixating on Guthrie. Trading his electric guitar for an acoustic one, he spent months in Minneapolis, performing in clubs, preparing himself for the trip east.

Going to New York rather than rival music center Los Angeles was a given, he says, "because everything I knew came out of New York. I listened to the Yankees games on the radio, and the Giants and the Dodgers. All the radio programs, like 'The Fat Man,' the NBC chimes—would be from New York. So were all the record companies. It seemed like New York was the capital of the world."

Devouring Poetry

Dylan pursued his muse in New York with an appetite for anything he felt would help him improve his craft, whether it was learning old blues and folk songs or soaking up literature.

"I had read a lot of poetry by the time I wrote a lot of those early songs," he volunteers. "I was into the hard-core poets. I read them the way some people read Stephen King. I had also seen a lot of it growing up. Poe's stuff knocked me out in more ways that I could name. Byron and Keats and all those guys. John Donne.

"Byron's stuff goes on and on and on and you don't know half the things he's talking about or half the people he's addressing. But you could appreciate the language."

He found himself side by side with the Beat poets. "The idea that poetry was spoken in the streets and spoken publicly, you couldn't help but be excited by that," he says. "There would always be a poet in the clubs and you'd hear the rhymes, and [Allen] Ginsberg and [Gregory] Corso—those guys were highly influential."

Dylan once said he wrote songs so fast in the '60s that he didn't want to go to sleep at night because he was afraid he might miss one. Similarly, he soaked up influences so rapidly that it was hard to turn off the light at night. Why not read more?

"Someone gave me a book of Francois Villon poems and he was writing about hard-core street stuff and making it rhyme," Dylan says, still conveying the excitement of tapping into inspiration from 15th century France. "It was pretty staggering, and it made you wonder why you couldn't do the same thing in a song.

"I'd see Villon talking about visiting a prostitute and I would turn it around. I won't visit a prostitute, I'll talk about rescuing a prostitute. Again, it's turning stuff on its head, like 'vice is salvation and virtue will lead to ruin.'"

When you hear Dylan still marveling at lines such as the one above from Machiavelli or Shakespeare's "fair is foul and foul is fair," you can see why he would pepper his own songs with phrases that forever ask us to question our assumptions—classic lines such as "there's no success like failure and failure's no success at all," from 1965's "Love Minus Zero/No Limit."

As always, he's quick to give credit to the tradition.

"I didn't invent this, you know," he stresses. "Robert Johnson would sing some song and out of nowhere there would be some kind of Confucius saying that would make you go, 'Wow, where did that come from?' It's important to always turn things around in some fashion."

Exploring His Themes

Some writers sit down every day for two or three hours, at least, to write, whether they are in the mood or not. Others wait for inspiration. Dylan scoffs at the discipline of daily writing.

"Oh, I'm not that serious a songwriter," he says, a smile on his lips. "Songs don't just come to me. They'll usually brew for a while, and you'll learn that it's important to keep the pieces until they are completely formed and glued together."

He sometimes writes on a typewriter but usually picks up a pen because he says he can write faster than he can type. "I don't spend a lot of time going over songs," Dylan says. "I'll sometimes make changes, but the early songs, for instance, were mostly all first drafts."

He doesn't insist that his rhymes be perfect. "What I do that a lot of other writers don't do is take a concept and line I really want to get into a song and if I can't figure out for the life of me how to simplify it, I'll just take it all—lock, stock and barrel—and figure out how to sing it so it fits the rhyming scheme. I would prefer to do that rather than bust it down or lose it because I can't rhyme it."

Themes, he says, have never been a problem. When he started out, the Korean War had just ended. "That was a heavy cloud over everyone's head," he says. "The communist thing was still big, and the civil rights movement was coming on. So there was lots to write about.

"But I never set out to write politics. I didn't want to be a political moralist. There were people who just did that. Phil Ochs focused on political things, but there are many sides to us, and I wanted to follow them all. We can feel very generous one day and very selfish the next hour."

Dylan found subject matter in newspapers. He point to 1964's "The Lonesome Death of Hattie Carroll," the story of a wealthy

Baltimore man who was given only a six-month sentence for killing a maid with a cane. "I just let the story tell itself in that song," he says. "Who wouldn't be offended by some guy beating an old woman to death and just getting a slap on the wrist?"

Other times, he was reacting to his own anxieties.

"A Hard Rain's A-Gonna Fall" helped define his place in pop with an apocalyptic tale of a society being torn apart on many levels.

I heard the sound of a thunder, it roared out a warnin'
Heard the roar of a wave that could drown the whole world.
Heard one hundred drummers whose hands were a-blazin'
Heard ten thousand whisperin' and nobody listenin' . . .
And it's a hard rain's a-gonna fall.

The song has captured the imagination of listeners for generations, and like most of Dylan's songs, it has lyrics rich and poetic enough to defy age. Dylan scholars have often said the song was inspired by the Cuban missile crisis.

"All I remember about the missile crisis is there were bulletins coming across on the radio, people listening in bars and cafes, and the scariest thing was that cities, like Houston and Atlanta, would have to be evacuated. That was pretty heavy.

"Someone pointed out it was written before the missile crisis, but it doesn't really matter where a song comes from. It just matters where it takes you."

His Constant Changes

Dylan's career path hasn't been smooth. During an unprecedented creative spree that resulted in three landmark albums ("Bringing It All Back Home," "Highway 61 Revisited" and "Blonde on Blonde") being released in 15 months, Dylan reconnected with the rock 'n' roll of his youth. Impressed by the energy he felt in the Beatles and desiring to speak in the musical language of his generation, he declared his independence from folk by going electric at the Newport Folk Festival in 1965.

His music soon became a new standard of rock achievement, influencing not only his contemporaries, including the Beatles, but almost everyone to follow.

The pressure on him was soon so intense that he went underground for a while in 1966, not fully resuming his career until the mid-'70s when he did a celebrated tour with the Band and then recorded one of his most hailed albums, "Blood on the Tracks." By the end of the decade, he confused some old fans by turning to brimstone gospel music.

There were gems throughout the '70s and '80s, but Dylan seemed for much of the '90s to be tired of songwriting, or, maybe, just tired of always being measured against the standards he set in the '60s.

In the early '90s he seemed to find comfort only in the rhythm of the road, losing himself in the troubadour tradition, not even wanting to talk about songwriting or his future. "Maybe I've written enough songs," he said then. "Maybe it's someone else's turn."

Somehow, however, all those shows reignited the songwriting spark—as demonstrated in his Grammy-winning "Time Out of Mind" album in 1997; the bittersweet song from the movie "Wonder Boys," "Things Have Changed," that won an Oscar in 2001 for best original song; and his heralded 2001 album, "Love and Theft." He spent much of last year working on a series of autobiographical chronicles. The first installment is due this fall from Simon & Schuster.

But nowhere, perhaps, is Dylan's regained passion more evident than in his live show, where he has switched primarily from guitar to electric keyboard and now leads his four-piece band with the intensity of a young punk auteur.

Dylan—who has lived in Southern California since he and ex-wife Sara Lowndes moved to Malibu in the mid-'70s with their five children—was in Amsterdam to headline two sold-out concerts at a 6,000-seat hall. He does more than 100 shows a year.

The audience on the chilly winter night after our first conversation is divided among people Dylan's age who have been following his career since the '60s and young people drawn to him by his classic body of work, and they call out for new songs, not just the classics.

Refiguring the Melodies

Back at the hotel afterward, Dylan looks about as satisfied as a man with his restless creative spirit can be.

It's nearly 2 a.m. by now and another pot of coffee cools. He rubs his hand through his curly hair. After all these hours, I realize I haven't asked the most obvious question: Which comes first, the words or the music?

Dylan leans over and picks up the acoustic guitar.

"Well, you have to understand that I'm not a melodist," he says. "My songs are either based on old Protestant hymns or Carter Family songs or variations of the blues form.

"What happens is, I'll take a song I know and simply start playing it in my head. That's the way I meditate. A lot of people will look at a crack on the wall and meditate, or count sheep or angels or money or something, and it's a proven fact that it'll help them relax. I don't meditate on any of that stuff. I meditate on a song.

"I'll be playing Bob Nolan's 'Tumbling Tumbleweeds,' for instance, in my head constantly—while I'm driving a car or talking to a person or sitting around or whatever. People will think they are talking to me and I'm talking back, but I'm not. I'm listening to the song in my head. At a certain point, some of the words will change and I'll start writing a song."

He's slowly strumming the guitar, but it's hard to pick out the tune.

"I wrote 'Blowin' in the Wind' in 10 minutes, just put words to an old spiritual, probably something I learned from Carter Family records. That's the folk music tradition. You use what's been handed down. 'The Times They Are A-Changin'' is probably from an old Scottish folk song."

As he keeps playing, the song starts sounding vaguely familiar.

I want to know about “Subterranean Homesick Blues,” one of his most radical songs. The 1965 number fused folk and blues in a way that made everyone who heard it listen to it over and over. John Lennon once said the song was so captivating on every level that it made him wonder how he could ever compete with it.

The lyrics, again, were about a society in revolution, a tale of drugs and misuse of authority and trying to figure out everything when little seemed to make sense:

Johnny's in the basement
Mixing up the medicine
I'm on the pavement
Thinking about the government

The music too reflected the paranoia of the time—roaring out of the speakers at the time with a cannonball force.

Where did that come from?

Without pause, Dylan says, almost with a wink, that the inspiration dates to his teens. “It's from Chuck Berry, a bit of ‘Too Much Monkey Business’ and some of the scat songs of the '40s.”

As the music from the guitar gets louder, you realize Dylan is playing one of the most famous songs of the 20th century, Irving Berlin's “Blue Skies.”

You look into his eyes for a sign.

Is he writing a new song as we speak?

“No,” he says with a smile. “I'm just showing you what I do.”

JESSICA HOPPER

Punk Is Dead! Long Live Punk!

A Report on the State of Teen Spirit from the Mobile Shopping Mall That Is the Vans Warped Tour

In the words of my friend J. R. Nelson, a local punk writer, "Teenagers are geniuses. I think the teenage me, the infantile and deeply stupid suburban milk baby who resented the entire world and just wanted a pair of Air Revolutions because they were expensive, was the purest me to ever grace this rotating shit orb."

Teenagers are also the most powerful audience in America, and this summer the Vans Warped Tour—which began June 25 in Houston and ends today, August 20, in Boston—celebrated ten years of unwavering devotion to this principle. At each stop anywhere from 10,000 to 30,000 teenagers converged on a parking lot, a stadium, or an amphitheater, wading deep into the froth of pop-cultural commerce that they drive with their fickle tastes. In exchange for the $18 to $30 that a Warped ticket cost, depending on the venue—not bad at all for five dozen bands—the sunburned throngs got eight hours of accessible punk, hardcore, and hip-hop.

But I don't think any impartial observer could conclude that Warped is first and foremost about the music. It's about teenagers and their disposable income. Punk in its primal form is of course a deeply anticommercial genre, but Warped has turned money into the medium of cultural affiliation here, as it already was everywhere else. What's being sold is an entrée into punk, and most of the fans are too new to the music's ideals to understand that they're buying a version of fuck-all rebellion that's been repackaged by businesspeople. Or maybe they do understand, and they come because they think it's the only version left. Warped is a mammoth shopping and marketing experience, a towering conglomerated product of the Clear Channel Age, and though the music is the initial draw, purchases are the way the kids express themselves to themselves, to the bands, and to each other.

Look no further than the Casualties' merch tent, with its 24 T-shirt designs, two styles of handkerchief, and three different hats. A day at Warped is about kids saying "I love you" to their favorite bands, with cash in hand—and on a scale that boggles the mind. We're a long way from the Fireside Bowl, which is the kind of punk dive many Warped acts came up playing, sometimes to only 20 or 30 kids at a time. Selling a handful of seven-inches for gas money isn't gonna cut it if you're touring as part of an operation that requires a fleet of ten tractor-trailers, a hundred tour buses and vans, 11 sound systems, a full-time on-site doctor and massage therapist, and a catering service that can handle two hot meals a day for 650 to 800 people. On July 24, the day Warped stopped at the Tweeter Center in Tinley Park, the band Taking Back Sunday grossed $20,000 in T-shirt sales alone.

I spent a few weeks on the 2004 Warped Tour, doing research for a book and hanging out with my boyfriend, who was performing. I got to spend a lot of time among the genius teenagers—the fans' average age seemed to be about 16. I remember 16 as a pretty grim year, but from the safe distance of a decade or so, 16-year-olds are completely fascinating. I was surrounded by thousands upon thousands of kids, a rushing tide of adolescent self-concept run riot, of bad tribal tattoos and rapturous infatuations and questionable hairstyles, all reeking of the pungent desire to simultaneously transgress and fit in perfectly.

This unself-conscious incoherence is a magnificent thing to behold. These kids all seemed to have a flawless idea of who they were—or who they wanted to seem to be, with their carefully arranged ensembles of brand names, slogans, and symbols—and absolutely no idea how they actually appeared. I saw boys milling around a San Diego sports pavilion parking lot, chewing on corn dogs and wearing mesh-back caps reading "My Balls Itch" at 11 AM on a Sunday. I saw a girl with the name of every act on the tour written in pen down the legs of her jeans—apparently signifying an impulse to identify with simply being at a "punk concert" more than loyalty to any of the actual bands. None of this, of course, was any less honest for being so obviously calculated—even when you're a teenager faking it, approximating a borrowed notion of cool, you're still bound to be more real, more transparent, and more vulnerable than any adult.

The second thing you notice at Warped—after the tens of thousands of kids—is the din. At any given moment there were at least four bands playing on the sprawling carnival midway of the concert campus. Most festivals make do with a single main stage and one or two distraction stages, but Warped was operating four main stages, four secondary stages, and a handful of stages-in-name-only—usually just a canopy in front of a van or a strip of grass between a set of PA speakers. The Brian Stage and the Teal Stage were for the headliners—and when a band on Brian finished its set, another band cranked up on Teal within three minutes. You could watch NOFX, the Alkaline Trio, the Sounds, and Yellowcard back-to-back simply by ping-ponging 100 feet to the left or right. Next year's headliners apparent (Rufio, My Chemical Romance, the Casualties) played on the Maurice Stage and the Volcom-sponsored stage, also side by side. Shunted out into the general population, next to the merch booths, were smaller elevated stages sponsored by Smartpunk, Punkrocks.net, and Ernie Ball. The Hurley/Kevin Says stage, barely a stage at all, had a ground-level linoleum floor and yellow caution tape strung along the front.

With so many bands playing at once, not even the most dedicated fan could see everything. Like a shopping mall or a giant punk-rock supermarket, the concert campus was designed to keep customers circulating, to induce them to check out every tent and booth at least once. Warped has even developed an ingenious strategy to bring the kids in early and keep them all day—the lineup of set times was different at every stop. Though technically a headliner, Bad Religion might have been playing at noon rather than taking the day's last slot at 7:30 PM. Thursday might have been slated for 1 PM or 5:15 PM, and you couldn't know till you got past the gate. So you'd show up at 11 in the morning and find out that your two favorite bands were going on at noon and 6 PM. What to do with the hours in between? There were band booths and label booths. There were good-cause booths: PETA, the Syrentha Savio Endowment (breast cancer awareness), Take Action! (progressive activism and "personal empowerment"). And then there were booths for the likes of Slim Jims (free wristbands and meat sticks!), Cingular Wireless (plastic gems and band stickers to decorate your cell phone!), and Dodge (custom racing cars in a showroom tent!). You could get your merch, purse, or person autographed, sign up for 100 different mailing lists, try out a bass or guitar, get your hair shaved into a Mohawk for free, or chew some complimentary Wrigley's Winterfresh gum. You could also buy stuff: sneakers, a skateboard deck, a hot dog, a hemp necklace, lemonade, band stickers or pins, spiked leather wristbands, thong underwear, a furry neon belt, sunglasses, a pizza from Domino's, a shirt that said "I'm sick and tired of white girls."

The hip-hop tent, dubbed the Code of the Cutz Stage, offered the only respite from the ever-present feeling of being marketed to. The dozen or so acts in the rotating daily lineup often left the stage, rubbing elbows with the crowd, or ventured outside the tent, mike in hand—I saw Connecticut rapper ADM (from the duo Glue) holding forth from atop the nearby picnic tables. It's not like there was no selling going on here, but it wasn't the faceless, focus-grouped variety: the Code of the Cutz performers frequently hawked their own CDs and shirts outside the tent after their sets. They were also pushing some of the most aggressive political agendas on the tour. NOFX, masterminds of Rock Against Bush, may pause between songs to wish Dick Cheney a heart attack, and Yellowcard may beg kids to get off their asses and vote, but those gestures seem rote next to Non-Phixion freestyling on the human impact of unfair drug-sentencing laws or Immortal Technique calling Condi Rice "the new age Sally Hemings."

On July 20 in Milwaukee, I hung out with a friend who ran the Alternative Press autograph booth while he got ready for a Taking Back Sunday signing. (The band's sets were always so mobbed that I never managed to see them from less than three-quarters of a mile away, but I did hear that TBS's kickball team with Thursday—aptly named Taking Back Thursday—was the one to beat on this year's tour.) My friend set up stools, laid out fresh Sharpies, stacked posters into huge piles, and shooed too-eager fans back into the quarter-mile line. In front was a boy in a homemade Taking Back Sunday T-shirt: with colored markers he'd written the date, the band's name, some lyrics, and the name of the venue in careful capitals, and along the bottom edge in alternating colors was a repeated rickrack ribbon of "Taking Back Sunday * Vans Warped Tour * Taking Back Sunday * Vans Warped Tour." The homemade Warped Commemorative Shirt, Pants, or Hat was common enough to be a phenomenon on the tour. That public display of affection, that preemptive sentimentality pivoting on this exact moment, is what emo has instilled in the culture of punk fandom: advance nostalgia for the peak experience.

That's not to say that Warped can't offer genuine peak experiences, even to a 27-year-old like me. In San Diego, I cried watching Patty Schemel play drums. She's a strong hitter with perfect placement, but more than that she plays with such joy that I could feel it myself. Schemel used to drum for Hole, but she's now with Juliette & the Licks, a new band fronted by Juliette Lewis—yes, that Juliette Lewis.

The audience at Warped, unlike the sausage party you get at a typical ground-level punk show, is half-female, maybe more. But in San Diego there were only seven women performing, spread across three bands. The Licks drew a screaming, girl-heavy crowd every time they played, though this was their first tour and they didn't even have a CD out yet. Between songs Lewis fell into a put-on honky-tonk drawl, yelling bons mots like "Aaawright!" and "This one is for the ladies!" and introducing the band at the top of her lungs. ("This is my drummah, Patty Schemel!") When I saw her she was wearing a couture T-shirt, a bikini, knee pads, and fingerless gloves, and her makeup was running with sweat. She grabbed her crotch, humped the monitors, threw the horned hand at the crowd, and assumed several different yoga positions. She's like Andrew W. K.'s spirit in Joan Jett's clothes. She's lithe and tough, a real performer—judging by how she moves, she's spent at least a third of her waking life with people staring at her.

In Los Angeles I watched the Mean Reds deliver what would turn out to be the rawest set I'd see on the tour. The Mean Reds are from Tucson and barely a year out of high school. It was only the sixth day of the tour, and they were already on "probation" for running their mouths onstage about what a sold-out capitalist-pig enterprise Warped is, how it isn't really punk, et cetera. Warped founder and figurehead Kevin Lyman in turn advised the boys to do their homework before letting fly with the rhetoric: Did they think for a minute that he'd invited all those sponsors along for the ride for any other reason than to defray the tour's enormous expenses and keep ticket prices sane? (You might assume a band would give these questions some thought before committing to a couple months on the tour.)

The Mean Reds are off the Richter, bionically crazy, oblivious and obnoxious and out of control. They have all the fire of Nation of Ulysses, but instead of suits and manifestos, they have other people's Klonopin prescriptions and women's thrift-store blouses à la Bob Stinson. They look like scumbags who sleep in the desert. I'm not sure they have any idea what they're doing or how great it is. Halfway through their apocalyptic 25-minute set, I told the guy who runs their label that Anthony Anzalone, the singer, reminded me of Darby Crash. The label guy said, "He has no idea who Darby Crash is." He also told me that the band had gotten into music by listening to Nirvana—and that they were recently the subject of a seven-label bidding war but refused all offers.

By the time Warped reached Minneapolis, a little more than three weeks later, the Mean Reds had been kicked off the tour. Their labelmates the Rolling Blackouts had gotten the boot after their singer pissed next to a stage while another band was playing, and Anzalone pissed his pants during a Mean Reds set in solidarity. The Mean Reds are more like the Warped audience than they know—confused, idealistic, angry, and furiously trying to slap the world awake and tell it who they think they are.

When I saw the band in LA, Anzalone was filthy, his sweat making bright stripes in the layer of dirt caked to his skin—he'd made a vow that he wouldn't shower until the band was off the tour, which at the time was still supposed to mean another month and a half. He was shirtless, covered in cuts, and wearing swim trunks, boat shoes, and a wrinkled women's vest with gold anchors on it. He rolled in the grass in front of the stage, right under the yellow caution-tape barrier and into the crowd. The security staff watched with alarm as this yawping kid, pink faced and exploding, writhed at our feet, humping the grass, grabbing ankles, and screaming, "Holla! Playa! Holla! Playa!"

Between songs he contended with the Winterfresh gum camper van 30 feet away, staffed by a chipper woman who leapt into the brief lulls in the Mean Reds' set to announce, via her large vehicle-mounted PA, that "Fresh breath and fresh music go together!" Anzalone glanced hatefully at the truck and passed the mike, interviewing the girls in the front row: "What does punk rock mean to you? What is punk rock about for you?"

A Latina no older than 15 with red-streaked hair and matching red bands on her braces answered, "Punk rock is about being who you are and doing what you want." The rest of the small audience, mostly older punks and industry folks, clapped.

ANDREW HULTKRANS

Revolution Blues

SHIT.

Arthur lit the hash pipe. Across the dark storage closet, Self's eyes echoed the flare, the corona receding concentrically into his deep canine pupils.

Neil Fucking Young. Big, cock-eyed, Indian-ass motherfucker. Look like a damn axe murderer. Cracked fucking smile of his. Why'd I tell him he could bring that wannabe dude up here. Calls him "Wizard" or some shit. Says he got some songs. On some freestyle poetry trip. Says he wants me to hook him up with Holzman. Shit. Stupid scarecrow canuck. He oughta know I been trying to get out from under Holzman ever since I signed with the dude. Got three albums worth with the new cats and I ain't giving Holzman jack. Can pucker up and kiss my black ass, what I say. Shit.

Arthur hit the pipe again, holding the lighter on in front of him as he blew smoke rings at Self. The Job tray, one of those. Art Nouveau trips, undulated beneath his gaze. The small flame played on the foil holding the brown lump of hash, a turd in a golden blanket. Some distended nuggets of Cap'n Crunch floated in the cereal bowl. He paddled them about with his spoon, an armada of orange sponges on a cruel white sea, breathing, drowning. Three tabs left. How long had he been in here? He flicked the lighter again, his nail on the wheel to avoid the burn, and looked at Self, who mewled quizzically. Still had food in his bowl. Under two days, then. He'd gone longer. Michael had told him about that film they made at the house right before he bought it. *The Trip*. Peter Fonda on his first dose, flipping out, running from the acid monster, hiding in this closet.

Punk motherfucker. Peter Fonda's a *Leave It to Beaver* hippie. Don't know jack about acid. That Hopper cat, though, is stone evil. I fumigated the place just knowing he was in here. Hanging with that midget Polanski and his Barbie-doll wife. On some devil trip. Fucking with runaways, Rock Hudson. I warned Bryan not to fuck with those people. *Don't you ever tell me you went up there ever again, you hear me?* I told him. Dennis Wilson? Shit. Dude's a clapped-out penis with legs, I told him. Walking syphilitic choad. His face even look like a dick. Not like his brother. Brian's straight-up honky. Fat, doughy, pie-eating motherfucker. Ain't nobody whiter than Brian Wilson.

Arthur heard the metallic churn of Neil's hearse straining up Mulholland. The house was at the top of Lookout Mountain, top of LA, top of the world. Everyone's car had trouble with the last mile. Freaks and sightseers were always knocking on Arthur's door for a jug of water to cool their overheated engines. He hated that. He moved up here to escape the leaking cesspool of the city below. And now they were coming up, after him, in their steaming, gasping tanks, trying to drag him down, take him away.

Shit. I don't want to listen to no dopey hippie talking smack. Get enough of that jive on the Strip. Peace and love flower-power bullshit. Them motherfuckers need to get themselves a job, join the Peace Corps, something. *Revolution*, they say. Shit. If there were a real revolution all these trust fund babies be crapping in their drawers, whining for Mommy. They need to get a job, get some talent, or shut up. Even the musicians starting to piss me off. That wannabe Morrison up here at my pool, loaded on ten thousand mics, wagging his silly pink dick at my neighbors. No fucking respect. "We want the world and we want it now"? Shit. He just want some teenage pussy. I had to get my shotgun to run his ass off my property. I'm a country boy. Nobody gonna expose his shit to my neighbors. I don't care who he is. Lizard King, my ass. He just a smelly cracker drunk in crusty leather pants. Ain't changed trou since he was a broke-ass "poet" sleeping on Venice Beach. Him and Manzarek were on my dick for two years on the Strip. Said they wanted to sound just like me. I get them a deal with Holzman and now Morrison's fat face is on every cover of *Teen Tiger* whatever *Beat*. Fucking pin-up. Got those Valley girls creaming in their shorts. Punk motherfucker. I put him on and he comes up here and flashes my neighbors. Shoulda smoked the clown right then. I told Bryan if he *ever* brought him up here again . . .

The hearse was in the driveway. Arthur heard fatigued cylinders popping and dying as the engine wound down. Doors slammed. The men were cackling about something. "Ar-thur," Neil's loopy voice called from outside, doppleringthrough the walls and into his head. "You in there?" Arthur's bowels tightened. He remained silent. Self growled, suspicious. "I brought my pal up, like I said. Gonna jam. He's got some things he wants to play for you." The two men entered the house, shutting the large oak door behind them. Neil called again. "Ar-thur, where the hell are ya?" Guitar cases thumped to the floor, muffled strings resonating from the impact. Inside the closet, to their right, Self barked. Arthur grabbed his collar and held him down. "You in *there*, man? In the *closet*? What kind of trip are you on? C'mon out. I want you to meet the Wizard." To the other man, he mock whispered, "Arthur's *pa-ra-noid*." Neil rapped Bo Diddley on the closet door. Self barked again, menacingly.

Arthur choked his collar, muting the sound to a strangled yelp. "I ain't coming out. That cat can play his shit through the door. I don't wanna hang with nobody right now."

Arthur pet Self to calm him. Hit the hash pipe, exhaled toward the door. A different voice—spaced, unctuous—wafted into the closet. "Hey, brother. You're the Love man. I'm a love man, too. I'm your kind. All is all and everything you could love or be. All is now and now is all in my heart, can you see? Dig, man. Never say never to always. C'mon out and let me lay my songs on you."

Self tugged at his collar, growling toward the door. "Naw, man. I'm staying put. You just play your shit and I'll listen. See what I can do." Neil muttered something about "Arthur's isolation trip." Said we should do as he says. Arthur's kind of a bad dude, Neil said. Ornery. Best not to mess with him.

Arthur heard guitar cases opening and the two men sitting down in the foyer besides the door. Tuning. One of them fired a joint. "Let's warm up with that song I showed you at Denny's place," Neil said to the Wizard. "Arthur, dig. This is one of my new ones, not for the Springfield. Gonna record it myself." Neil strummed a midtempo, two-chord trip. Something about a chick. Then the chorus came. "Down by the river . . . I shot my baby." Sick motherfucker, Arthur thought. Tell just by looking at him. The Wizard plunked along on one note, a private rhythm. "Dead . . . shot her dead." Damn, Arthur thought, why I even let these fools in my house? Why do I even *know* Neil Young? Motherfucker drives a *hearse*. Shit. The song droned on and on. For a while both guitars were playing one note, in some kind of demented, unintentional syncopation. Neil shot his baby again and again, his voice warbling cracked, triumphant glee. The song imploded slowly and died. "Whaddaya think, Arthuuurrrr?" Neil asked, raising his voice as if calling across a canyon. A wave of nausea rose from Arthur's intestines. Cold sweat. Acid shivers. "That's some heavy shit, Neil," Arthur answered, coughing. "I ain't down with killing women, but whatever your trip is, man."

Before Neil could answer, the Wizard strummed a choppy, strident progression. Bounced and lurched like an old hooptie. No sense of rhythm. Between beats, he began to sing:

Cease to exist
Just come and say you love me
Give up your world
C'mon you can see

I'm your kind, I'm your kind
You can see

His voice wasn't bad. A sandy, nasal rasp. White boy blues, Arthur thought. Lyrics are straight ga-ga bullshit, though.

Submission is a gift
Go on, give it to your brother
Love and understanding is for one another
I'm your kind, I'm your kind
I'm your mind
I'm your brother

Neil soloed throughout, punctuating lines with staccato notes and bends. Like a spastic B. B. King, Arthur thought. The song wound down with the Wizard chanting, "I am the real . . . thing . . . oo mau ma mau mau oo mau ma mau mau" in a disembodied whisper. Arthur shuddered. He didn't want to even shake this dude's hand. Wanted him out, soon as possible. Without waiting for a response from his host, the Wizard segued into some whacked out nursery-rhyme.

I am a mechanical man
And I do the best I can
Because I have my family
I am a mechanical boy
I am my mother's toy
And I play in the backyard sometimes

I had a little monkey
And I sent him to the country
And I fed him ginger bread
Along came a choo-choo
And knocked my monkey koo-koo
And now my monkey's dead

Neil was giggling now, unable to play. "Told you, Arthur. He just makes this crazy stuff up as he goes along. Never the same trip twice. He's like a living poet." The Wizard had already changed tunes, this one a draggy blues about LA.

Sick city, yeah, restless people
From the sick city burnt their houses down
To make the sky look pretty

This town is killing me
Got to put an end to this restless misery

I hear that Laurel Canyon is full of famous stars
But I hate them worse than lepers and I'll kill them in their cars

Neil chuckled at this last couplet. Arthur could picture his goofy grin, head bobbing. In the closet shafts of light cut through the vertical edges of the door. The sun had shifted, beaming through the wide window on the west side of the foyer, shining directly on the door. Dust motes passed through the rays, forming shapes from Arthur's mind. Self was anxious, walking in circles, grumbling. Arthur heard Neil get up as the Wizard nattered on. "Got any wine, man? I'm gonna check the kitchen. You just keep on listening. He can go on forever. Hope you dig it." Arthur heard footsteps fade down the stairs, Neil whistling as he walked. I just gotta tune this creepy dude out, Arthur thought. Tell Neil to take his ass out of here as soon as he gets back.

The Wizard put down his guitar with a hollow thump, stood up, and moved closer to the closet door. He spoke, addressing Arthur in forced collusion. "When the revolution comes . . . " Shit. Here we go. ". . . hairy locusts will emerge from the pit and take over the world. The Beatles left me a message, on the White Album. John the Revelator is John Lennon. Revelation 9 is Revolution 9. Dig?" Arthur shook. Goddamn freaks are eating my world, he thought. "But first the Black man has to rise up against the rich white piggies. Kill them in their homes. Paint white walls with their blood. It was written. When the Black man rises the revolution begins. The locusts wait in the desert, in the hole that has no bottom." Redneck lunatic. I didn't sign up for this shit. He flashed on the drinking fountains in Memphis, when he was a boy. His stomach wrestled itself. Self sensed his master's rage, emitting a constant guttural growl, an idling engine at the starting line. "Neil tells me you're a spade," the Wizard continued, his voice louder, soured with contempt. "Tells me you look just like Jimi Hendrix. We need you boys to rise up and lead the revolution, dig? You're the vanguard. You and the Panthers. Gotta rise up and kill the piggies. C'mon, Black man, rise up!" The Wizard was bellowing now, stomping the floor like a Baptist preacher. "C'mon now, RISE! RISE! RISE!"

Bullshit. In one fluid motion, Arthur struck the lighter, grabbed his shotgun, bucked the door and fired. The kick blew the men apart. Arthur reeled backward as the Wizard, a scrawny little freak with a greasy brown beard, fell to the floor, blood from his heart pumping onto the foyer, coursing down the stairs. Self leapt onto the body, sniffing for signs of life. There were none. The Wizard's blue eyes stared at the ceiling, blank, elsewhere. Neil ran up the stairs from the kitchen, bleating like a toothless grandmother, unable to form words. As he turned the corner to the foyer, he heard Arthur shouting.

"I ain't *your kind* and you ain't *my brother*!" Revolution. Shit. Got your revolution right here. Neil saw Arthur holding the shotgun, hovering over the lifeless Wizard. "And *I* do not look like Jimi Hendrix. Jimi Hendrix looks like *me*. Motherfucker."

GREIL MARCUS

The Lost Boy

Buddy Holly walked into the room sideways. In terms of pure power he can't stand up to those with whom he's most often linked as a pioneer of rock 'n' roll: Elvis Presley, Little Richard, and Chuck Berry. He recorded nothing as immediately overwhelming—nothing that so forced an absolute confrontation between performer and listener—as "Hound Dog," "Tutti Frutti," or "Johnny B. Goode." The most musically extreme record of Holly's time was Little Richard's "Ready Teddy": Elvis can't keep up with Little Richard's version, but Holly, despite guitar playing that almost changes the sound of the song entirely, can't keep up with Elvis.

Buddy Holly shied away from the violence implicit in rock 'n' roll as it first made itself known, and from the hellfire emotionalism on the surface of the music. He was a rockabilly original, but unlike Gene Vincent—or Carl Perkins, Jerry Lee Lewis, or Sun label wildmen like Billy Lee Riley and Sonny Burgess, who after the release of his "Red Headed Woman" dyed his hair red and bought a red suit and a red Cadillac—Holly looked for space in the noise. He built his music around silences, pauses, a catch in the throat, a wink.

"That'll Be the Day" may be a very hard-nosed record, but its intensity is eased by its brightness—by the way it courts the prettiness that took over later Holly tunes like "Everyday," or even

"Oh Boy" or "Rave On." "Hound Dog" aims for the monolithic, and falls short; "That'll Be the Day" is all pluralism, fully realized. The singer is acting out his role in a dozen accents; like Rod Stewart combing his hair a thousand ways in "Every Picture Tells a Story," he's talking to the mirror, rehearsing what he's going to say, writing it down. He's saying it on the phone while the phone's still ringing at the other end, going over how perfectly he said what he meant to say after he's said it, savoring the memory. Holly is reaching for Elvis's roughness, but even as he does so he communicates doubt that he can carry it off—or that anyone should.

And that's why "That'll Be the Day" is a more convincing record than "Hound Dog"—as Bobby Vee put it, thinking back to first hearing the record on the radio in Fargo, North Dakota, in 1957, when he was 14-year-old Bob Veline: "To me it was the most original, fresh, unique record I ever heard—and I was right, it was."

Holly could be utterly sure of his self-doubt; Elvis couldn't be as sure of his arrogance, and so he muffles it with a self-mocking laugh. In that part of himself that was addressing "Hound Dog" to the world at large, to the world that mocked him, you can hear Elvis meaning every word of "Hound Dog"; in the part of himself that was addressing the woman in the song, he's just kidding. Buddy wasn't kidding on "That'll Be the Day." Holly's performance is tougher—just as "Well . . . All Right," a 1958 single with no orchestration other than acoustic guitar, bass, and fluttered cymbals, is tougher still.

Holly's almost frightening sincerity was cut with playfulness, a risk-free sense of fun, and an embrace of adolescent or even babyish innocence that was likely as calculated as his famous hiccups. Without that innocence and playfulness, his sincerity could have led him to take himself so seriously that today his music might sound hopelessly overblown; without his sincerity, many of his songs would now sound moronic. Instead he so often struck a perfect balance.

"Anarchy had moved in," Nik Cohn wrote of the '50s in *Awopbopaloobop Alopbamboom*—the first good book on rock 'n' roll, the book Cohn first called *Pop from the Beginning*. "For thirty years you couldn't possibly make it unless you were white, sleek, nicely spoken, and phony to your toenails—suddenly now you could be black, purple, moronic, delinquent, diseased, or almost anything on earth, and you could still clean up." What Buddy Holly was saying, what he was acting out, was that you could also be ordinary.

A photograph was taken in Lubbock, Texas, in 1955, on the occasion of Elvis Presley's second visit to Buddy Holly's hometown. In this picture, Elvis, surrounded by teenage girls and boys and children, looks bigger than anyone else: taller, wider, taking up more psychic space. Even with a dumb, open-mouthed look on his face, you can feel his glow.

On Presley's far left, just peeking into the frame, is an 18-year-old Buddy Holly, the only male figure (among 30-odd people in the picture) wearing glasses, somewhere between geek and nerd, looking curious. You would never pick him out of this crowd—or would you? No, probably not: there's no aura around his body, no portent in his posture, not even any obvious desire in his eyes. Just that curiosity: but even as he pokes his head forward for a closer look, he holds his body back. His curiosity is a form of hesitation, a drama of doubt. That quality of doubt is what gives the Buddy Holly in this picture the interest he has—and the longer you look at the picture, the less stable it appears to be. Who can identify with who? Who would want to identify with the nobody? But who can really identify with the god—and in this black and white photo, no matter what the expression on his face, it's plain a god is in the room. Elvis Presley and Buddy Holly, sharing the same time and space—they're both magnets, Elvis the black hole, Holly merely earthly gravity.

It was Buddy Holly's embodiment of ordinariness that allowed him to leave behind not only a body of songs, but a personality—

as his contemporaries Elvis, Chuck Berry, Little Richard, and Jerry Lee Lewis did, and Carl Perkins, Danny and the Juniors, Larry Williams, Fats Domino, the Monotones, Arlene Smith, or Clyde McPhatter did not.

The personality was that of the guy you passed in the hall in your high school every day. He might be cool; he might be square. He might be the guy who slammed your locker shut every time you opened it, but the guy who did it as a laugh, as a version of a pat on the back, a "Hey, man." He might be the guy who got his own locker slammed shut in his own face, and not in fun. Whoever he was, he was familiar. He was not strange; he was not different; he did not speak in unknown tongues, or commune with secret spirits.

Except that he did. "Well . . . All Right" is not just a good song, or a great recording; with a quietness that is also a form of loudness, the drum sticks moving over the cymbals like wind on water, the feel of death in the lack of any physical weight to the sound, the sense of a threat in every promise, "Well . . . All Right" is also the casting of a spell, but no one ever seemed less like a sorcerer than Buddy Holly.

"An obvious loser," Nik Cohn said. "He was the patron saint of all the thousands of no-talent kids who ever tried to make a million dollars. He was founder of a noble tradition." What Cohn is describing is how the gawky, wide-eyed Buddy Holly who Gary Busey summoned up for *The Buddy Holly Story* in 1978—someone who looks as if he's about to fall down every time he does that Buddy Holly move where he folds up his knees like a folding chair—is as believable as the cool, confident, hipster Buddy Holly that Marshall Crenshaw plays at the end of *La Bamba* in 1987, performing "Crying, Waiting, Hoping" on that last stage in Clear Lake, Iowa, then waving Ritchie Valens onto the plane: "Come on—the sky belongs to the stars."

If Holly looked like an ordinary teenager, on the radio he came across as one. His presence on stage, on the airwaves, seemed more accidental that willful. From his first professional recordings, the mostly muffled numbers cut in Nashville in

1956, to the Clovis, New Mexico, sessions produced by Norman Petty in 1957, on through the soulful solo demos he made in New York in late 1958 and into the next year, the most glamorous element of Holly's career was the plane crash that ended it—on February 3, 1959, leaving his 22-year-old body in an Iowa cornfield along with those of 17-year-old Ritchie Valens and 29-year-old J. P. Richardson, the Big Bopper.

So Buddy Holly entered history differently from other rock 'n' roll heroes—and, somehow, his ordinariness has carried over into the way in which one might encounter people whose lives brushed his. Some years ago, on a panel in New Orleans, David Adler, author of *The Life and Cuisine of Elvis Presley*, shocked me and everyone else in the room with the story of how, during his research in Tupelo, Mississippi, he met a woman who was in the Presleys' one-room house when Elvis Presley was born—and he believed her because of the way she described how the shoebox containing the still-born body of Elvis's twin Jesse Garon was resting on the kitchen table.

A gasp went up. We were in the presence of someone who had been in the presence of someone who had been present when an event took place that ultimately would change the world—and leave all of us present in that world different than we would have otherwise been if this event had not taken place.

But nothing like that feeling attaches itself to the story I heard when, without asking, I found myself listening to a woman tell how, missing Buddy Holly's last concert as a 12-year-old because no one she knew was vulgar enough to go with her, she asked a friend to drive her to the site of the crash before the morning light was up, and how men with stretchers were still there when she arrived. Or listening to a woman who lives down the street from me in Berkeley describe how, as a girl, she witnessed the collision of two planes over Pacoima Junior High School, Ritchie Valens's alma mater, in 1957, a disaster that killed three students and that, at least until he climbed onto that Cessna at the little airport in Mason City, Iowa, left Ritchie Valens determined to stay out of the air if he could. Or listening in an Italian restaurant in New York in 1995 when, as if he'd never told the story before, Dion DiMucci quietly went through the details of the life-threatening conditions he and everyone else endured while traveling the upper Midwest on ruined buses for the Winter Dance Party tour in January and February 1959, and why he nevertheless gave up his seat on the plane that night. Or listening in San Francisco in 1970, as Bobby Vee told the story of how, when the news of the plane crash reached Fargo Senior High School the next morning, with everyone geared up for the show that evening, just over the state line in Moorhead, Minnesota, Bob Veline and his high school band, which lacked a name and had not yet played a single show, answered the call of the local promoter and, after rushing out to buy matching angora sweaters and 25-cent ties, and naming themselves the Shadows, took the stage that night along with those who were left.

Thus did he begin to tell his own part of the greater rock 'n' roll story: a story that—as Bob became one of various post-Holly Bobbys, made over on the terms of Holly's anybodyness, with anything that made this particular anybody unique air-brushed out—took the form of such first-rate teen-angst classics as "Take Good Care of My Baby," "It Might as Well Rain Until September," "The Night Has a Thousand Eyes," and, in 1962, as a shameless tribute, or an honest thank you, *Bobby Vee Meets The Crickets.* The plane crash gave Bob Veline his big break; as he saw it, it also gave him a legacy to honor, a mission to fulfill.

Because of the way Buddy Holly died—cut off in the bloom of youth, with his whole life ahead of him, chartering a plane because his clothes were filthy from the bus and he wanted to look good on stage, because he wanted to sleep for a few hours in a warm bed, and do a good show—he immediately became a mythic figure. A queer mythic figure: a mythic figure you could imagine talking to. One you could imagine listening to what you had to say.

But that sense of ordinariness in Buddy Holly is also ridiculous. It's ridiculous that a full-length biography—Philip Norman's 1996 *Rave On*—could be written about someone who never reached the age of 23, written without padding, without discographical pedanticism, quotidian minutiae, a potted social history of the 1950s, banal or for that matter profound musings on the emergence of the American teenager, rock 'n' roll, modern youth culture, or the meaning of the Alamo. And it's ridiculous that anyone could have left behind a body of work as rich as that Buddy Holly set down between the beginning 1957 and the end of 1958. But in that body of work is a story that can be told again and again without it ever being settled.

Some of the songs are obvious, despite a charm that isn't: "Everyday," "It Doesn't Matter Anymore," "Raining in My Heart," "It's So Easy," "Heartbeat." "Even the obvious beaters, things like 'Rave On' or 'Oh Boy,'" Nik Cohn wrote, "were Neapolitan flowerpots after 'Tutti Frutti.'" Cohn is right. But more of what Holly did is unlikely before it is anything else.

You could start with "Not Fade Away," probably the oddest Buddy Holly record of all. On paper, it's nothing but an underorchestrated Bo Diddley imitation. But as you hear it, no matter how many times you've heard it, it sounds nearly impossible. You can't date it by its sound, its style, the apparent recording technology. But while this is the Crickets, with Jerry Allison playing drums—or a cardboard box—Joe Mauldin bass, and Holly guitar, as they did on the leaping "That'll Be the Day," "Not Fade Away" is all stop-time, every build-up cut off and brought up short, the whole song starting up again, like the car it drops into the rhythm like a new dance step: "My love bigger than a Cadillac." With verbs evaporating out of the lyric, the thing feels less like any kind of pop song than a folk song, and less like the Rolling Stones's 1964 wailing-down-the-highway version, their first American single, than the Beatles's "Love Me Do," their first single anywhere, from 1962, which the late Ralph J. Gleason, music columnist for the *San Francisco Chronicle*, would refer to as "that Liverpool folk song," confusing some readers, like me, into wondering if perhaps it actually was.

With the hesitations in the beat, in the vocal, the recording is not easy to listen to, because it does not really make sense. It is absurd in the most wonderful way. Always, when people have talked about the 1920s and 1930s recordings Harry Smith brought together for his 1952 *Anthology of American Folk Music*—the likes of William and Versey Smith's "When That Great Ship Went Down," Dock Boggs's "Country Blues," or the Memphis Jug Band's "K. C. Moan"—they've found themselves drawn to the same phrase. "The music sounds as if it came out of the ground," they say, and that's exactly what "Not Fade Away" sounds like, which is to say that it also sounds more like flying saucer rock 'n' roll than Billy Lee Riley's "Flying Saucers Rock 'n' Roll."

Then there is "Peggy Sue," from 1957, and the 1958 home recording of "Peggy Sue Got Married." Here is where the ordinariness of the singer creates a unique kind of intimacy with the listener—even though the quiet, troubled, happy man in "Peggy Sue Got Married" is hardly the hard, even avenging man in "Peggy Sue," a man who refuses to explain himself and demands that you believe him anyway.

This man rides the coldness of the music, as cold in "Peggy Sue" as the music in "Peggy Sue Got Married" is warm: the battering, monochromatic tom-tom rumble from Jerry Allison that opens "Peggy Sue," named for Allison's girlfriend (when the song was written: the next year she was his wife, and 11 years later his ex-wife); the bass strum behind that; the instrument beneath both you can barely register. No leaps, no grand gestures, just a push head-down into the wind the song itself is making, and then that harsh, cruel guitar solo, emerging as inevitably as any in the music, and also a shock. The song is unexplainable, at least by me—but not by Jonathan Cott, writing the Buddy Holly chapter in *The Rolling Stone Illustrated History of Rock & Roll* in 1975.

"The women of '50s rock 'n' roll, about whom songs were written and to whom they were addressed," Cott says, "were as interchangeable as hurricanes or spring showers, Party Doll ornaments of the song. But with Peggy Sue, Buddy Holly created the first rock and roll folk heroine (Chuck Berry's Johnny B. Goode is her male counterpart). And yet it is difficult to say how he did it. Unlike the 'Sad-Eyed Lady of the Lowlands'—whom Bob Dylan fills in as he invents and discovers her—Peggy Sue is hardly there at all. Most '50s singers let it be known that they liked the way their women walked and talked; sometimes they even let on as to the color of their sweethearts' eyes and hair.

"But Buddy Holly didn't even give you this much information. Instead, he colluded with his listeners, suggesting that they imagine and create Peggy Sue *for him*."

Cott notes that Holly would later intensify this complicit relationship in "Peggy Sue Got Married," beseeching both his listeners and himself to keep secret what they both know to be true, as if by its revelation the rumor "heard from a friend" will irrevocably become fact. Holly cannot sing "You're the one," but "She's the one." Ultimately Peggy Sue, Holly's own creation, is as much of a mystery to him as anyone else. "He has become one of his own listeners," writes Cott, "as Peggy Sue vanishes, like Humbert Humbert's Lolita, into the mythology of American Romance."

Buddy Holly "suggested" that his listeners "imagine and create Peggy Sue for him," Cott says. The idea sounds so far-fetched, and yet in "Peggy Sue Got Married" it's literal: "I don't say / That it's true / I'll just leave that up to you."

And there are, finally, the remainder of Buddy Holly's last recordings, the solo pieces with guitar, acoustic or electric, that he taped in his and his wife Maria Elena's apartment in Greenwich Village in 1958—though the word *finally* seems wrong, because these are also the recordings that are most suggestive of the music Holly had yet to make, and the life he had yet to live. There is a version of Mickey and Sylvia's "Love Is Strange" that is more than anything strange—strangely abstract, so much so that the strings added after Holly's death let you imagine the singer resisting them in advance. Even odder, and far more affecting, is a reworking of Mickey and Sylvia's "Dearest," a composition that, written with Bo Diddley, is quiet, graceful, most of all a whisper—and, here, pure Holly, taken very slowly, as if the feeling the song calls up is so transporting that it would be a crime to let the song end. There is "Learning the Game," sung with tremendous confidence, the singer moving right into the music, riding the clipped guitar strum, no hesitation, no lingering—no speed, but no pauses, either. He never raises the tone, never increases the pressure.

And there is "Crying, Waiting, Hoping," overdubbed twice after Holly's death—in New York in 1959, leaving Holly kicking up the traces of his fate, and in Clovis in 1963 with the Fireballs, where there is no doubt that Holly has been in the ground for years. In the initial recasting, you can feel the seriousness of the composition, the great weight Holly gives the title words as the song opens. The melody is almost too sweet to bear. At the end, Holly repeats the title words again, isolating them from the rest of the music, as if they are a manifesto, a flag he's unfurling: "Crying—Waiting—Hoping"—the end.

It is this music that allows anyone to picture Buddy Holly in the years to come: to imagine his style deepening, his range increasing, his music taking shapes no one, not Holly, not his fans, could have predicted. When he died, Holly had plans for his own production company, publishing firm, management company, record label, all under the name Prism; the business cards were printed. He saw himself recording with Ray Charles, or making a gospel album with Mahalia Jackson. He was spending time in Village jazz clubs and coffeehouses, at the Village Vanguard, the Blue Note, the Bitter End, Café Bizarre; he'd registered at the Actor's Studio. But his career was slipping in late 1958. He and the Crickets had split up. The money he'd made, a fortune, was sitting in a bank in Clovis, New Mexico, and sitting on that money was producer and publisher Norman Petty, forcing Buddy Holly to live on loans from his wife's aunt. If you can see Buddy Holly as an entrepreneur in the music business, president of Prism Music, you can also see him, a year or two down the line, as a contract songwriter, side-by-side with Carole King, Gerry Goffin, Cynthia Weil, Barry Mann,

Ellie Greenwich, and Jeff Barry at Don Kirshner's Brill Building adjunct: Buddy Holly, like everyone else, writing songs for Bobby Vee.

But if you can see Holly in his cubicle in Aldon Music, you can also see him sitting in the audience at Folk City or the Gaslight—perhaps there to see the Texas folk singer Carolyn Hester, whom he'd backed on guitar in Norman Petty's studio in Clovis in 1958 on his own "Take Your Time" and other tunes, none of them released—but this night also watching Bob Dylan (who would himself back Hester on harmonica in 1961 for her third album, on Columbia, on "Come Back Baby," which Dylan would teach her) getting up out of the audience to sing "Handsome Molly" or "No More Auction Block."

And you can see Dylan back in the crowd a few minutes later, watching as Holly, whom Dylan would have noticed the minute he walked in, himself stood up to play "Not Fade Away," stamping his foot for the beat, or "Well . . . All Right," Dylan watching the smile on Holly's face for the "Well all right so I'm going steady / It's all right when people say / That those foolish kids can't be ready / For the love that comes their way" lines, Holly daring the hip crowd to laugh and no one daring to laugh, everyone frozen by the way Holly lets "the love that comes their way" drift into the smoke of its own air.

It's certain that in 1962 Bob Dylan would not have forgotten, as he would declare in 1998, when he accepted the Grammy for Album of the Year for *Time Out of Mind*, that on January 31, 1959, he was present in the Duluth Armory for Buddy Holly's third-to-last performance, and that, as he sat in the audience, as he told the nation and the world, "Buddy Holly looked right at me"—meaning that, on that night, Buddy Holly had passed on the secret of rock 'n' roll, of all music, of life itself, one avatar to another: a secret which, as of that night at the Grammys, Bob Dylan was plainly unready to pass on in turn.

CHRIS NORRIS

The Ghost of Saint Kurt

According to Japan's Shinto faith, when a person dies, his or her spirit passes into nature to reside in the air, water, and rocks. If the person has distinguished him- or herself in life, the spirit becomes a *kami*, a deity associated with powerful forces like wind and thunder. These deities can be endowed with completely opposite personalities—gentle or violent.

"[He] made women want to nurture and protect him," a friend, Carrie Montgomery, once said of Kurt Cobain. "He was a paradox in that way, because he also could be brutally and intensely strong, yet at the same time, he could appear fragile and delicate." The Japanese believe that after death the spirit is angry and defiled. Relatives perform rituals to pacify and purify it. Those who die happily, among their families, become revered ancestors. Those who die unhappily or violently—usually through murder or suicide—are called *yurei*, ghosts who wander about causing trouble. The ghosts of suicides are said to be the most dangerous.

She'll come back as fire, to burn all the liars, and leave a blanket of ash on the ground.—"Frances Farmer Will Have Her Revenge on Seattle" [Nirvana, *In Utero*, 1993]

In July 1989, a band recently signed to Seattle indie label Sub Pop appeared at a small New Jersey nightclub. They went on early, played to about 30 people, and, according to a witness, "just incinerated the place." The group had built a strong word-of-mouth following since the release of their first single the previous year, but for newcomers, the show was a revelation. "It was like, 'What the fuck?'" says the witness, Sonic Youth's Thurston Moore (who later helped the band sign to DGC). "Not only was every song crushingly great, but at the end, they just smashed their instruments and threw them into the audience. It seemed totally new."

To Moore, the trio looked like the demonic hick kids in the horror film *Children of the Corn*. "You know, long stringy hair, ragged flannel, and ripped dungarees." The 22-year-old singer's voice "had a teenage Lemmy quality [referring to the gristly, guttural Motörhead singer], and that band knew how to rock. It was so simple: the best parts of R.E.M., the Beatles, the Buzzcocks, Black Flag. But no band was doing that. Nobody in their *right mind* would reference R.E.M. or the Beatles then. But they did. And it worked."

You might say that. Within two years, Nirvana were the biggest rock band in the world; within three, the biggest of the decade; and within five, kaput. In that time, their small, skinny, singer/guitarist devised '90s rock and helmed a sweeping cultural change of style, attitude, and outlook. Then he ended his life.

Although some Shinto texts talk about the "High Plain of Heaven" or the "Dark Land," none provides any details about the afterlife. In Buddhism, the only true end of suffering is the attainment of total enlightenment. A peace beyond peace. A line in a recently published letter—sent to a friend in 1988 from a young blond punk rocker in Washington state—sounds, even today, far from peaceful and like anything but an ending. It announces, in bold block letters, OUR LAST AND FINAL NAME IS NIRVANA.

Kurt Cobain was many things while he was alive—punk, pop star, hero, victim, junkie, feminist, geek avenger, wiseass. But ten years after his death, he's something else entirely. He's a *ghost*. His songs play every so often on iPods, jukeboxes, at ball games.

An undiscovered one, "You Know You're Right," surfaced in 2002. The same year, his journals were published as a pricey coffee-table hardcover (*Journals*). Now there's a "classic alternative" radio format that may enshrine Nirvana as the new Led Zeppelin. But these flickers in the current pop world merely highlight his absence, reminding us of a figure who's becoming harder to see.

Cobain's career was short even by rock standards—three albums and out. He was, by his own admission, unprolific, and, after long battles with his former bandmates, his widow, Courtney Love, has established tight control over what remains of his recorded output. And although John Lennon, Jimi Hendrix, Jim Morrison, and other rock superstars died young, none had so much of the field to himself in his heyday or quite the exit strategy. Cobain's closest peer, Tupac Shakur, isn't a ghost. He's a full-time rap star. A workaholic in a medium where the tape's always running, he's still collaborating, topping charts, showing up in movies. And his postmortem role seems in many ways like wish fulfillment. "I got more to say," you can hear him taunting. "I'm gonna haunt you motherfuckers *forever*!" A video ("I Ain't Mad at Cha") that depicts him rapping in heaven was released just days after his death.

On the other hand, the bitter finality of Cobain's end became an indelible part of his story, like some sick MasterCard joke. (Debut album: $606.17. Remington 20-gauge: $308.37. Legend: Priceless.) No other chapter in pop music has so much darkness at its center. And no other artist still haunts us in such a powerful, subliminal way.

In a short speech he taped right after his best friend and bandleader died, Nirvana bassist Krist Novoselic advised fans, "Let's keep the music with us. We'll always have it forever." And he was right: The music speaks for itself. As a songwriter, Cobain was spookily brilliant. He had a way of making his offhand jokes and teen vernacular sound ancient and profound, with a melodic drama that verged on telekinesis. But this also had everything to do with who he was.

"There's part of him that was a cultural revolutionary and part of him that was a classic song craftsman," says Danny Goldberg, a former Nirvana manager and founder of Artemis Records. "This was someone who was inspired by the Melvins, but who listened a lot to the Beatles. He had that dual talent: an emotional cultural talent and a songwriting genius. Which is why people talk about John Lennon in a different tone of voice than Paul McCartney. Kurt was one of the masters of the craft, in addition to being a voice of adolescents of all ages."

Songs like "Pennyroyal Tea," "Heart-Shaped Box," "Come as You Are," "Smells Like Teen Spirit," and "In Bloom" will outlive us all. But those of us who are living now, who remember when Kurt Cobain the person was here living, talking, and creating—we experienced something else, too. We learned a story that has a certain beginning and a certain ending. And the fact is, Cobain's last work, which is now available worldwide on websites, isn't a song, drawing, or film. It's a piece of writing that reads, THIS NOTE SHOULD BE PRETTY EASY TO UNDERSTAND.

In April 1994, the mainstream media grappled with the death of an icon whose music they'd barely processed. Only two years earlier, *The New York Times* tried to get with the hip new thing by earnestly issuing a "grunge lexicon," concocted on the spot by a pranking Sub Pop receptionist. Back then, mainstream hoaxes were easier to pull, secrets easier to keep. Less than 10 percent of the population had Internet access. And the era's new, vaguely Brad Pitt-looking "it" boy—the Justin Timberlake of his time—occasionally wore black nail polish or a dress, dyed his hair with strawberry Kool-Aid, and sang, on MTV in prime time, lyrics like "Sell the kids for food" and "Nature is a whore."

But soon after he died, the media gave a specific cast to Cobain's quickly cooling image. The clips that played in the days after his death were from Nirvana's late-1993 MTV *Unplugged* appearance. They showed a frail 26-year-old who looked both much younger and much older, crouched over an acoustic guitar, clearly in misery. He was bathed in blue light and surrounded by lilies, the traditional American flower of death. The set, designed by Cobain, was specifically meant to resemble a funeral. Of the six cover songs he played, five mentioned death.

At the height of his notoriety, jazz great Charlie Parker complained that people were paying to see the world's most famous junkie. Cobain, among other things, is his generation's most famous suicide. "I mean, people die," says Moore. "But I can't think of too many musicians of his caliber and celebrity who died *that way*." When people heard of Cobain's death, they tended to have a two-part reaction, first to the death, then to the method. People who OD, drive drunk, or invite murder threats have a pretty reckless disregard for their lives and the lives of their loved ones. But Cobain's last act was different.

Goldberg remembers him as "the typical artistic control freak, someone who edited his home video meticulously." But years later, it's easy to wonder whether he was a control freak on a level few then imagined. What if he was so attentive, so farsighted in his performance art, that he somehow, maybe unconsciously, had his whole curtain call plotted out? There he is in the last shot of the "Teen Spirit" video. An eerie yellow blur, too close to the camera to be in focus, he scream-sings those last words: *a denial, a denial, a denial*. . . . As Dave Grohl's drums crash to a halt, he holds that last word for a drawn-out, head-quivering note. Then suddenly, viciously, he snaps his mouth shut. The end.

So how does it feel now, when you're driving down the road at night, past Blockbuster and Applebee's, and, just as Trapt's "Headstrong" fades out on the radio, you hear those first strums of "Smells Like Teen Spirit"? Is it awesome? Does it *totally fucking rock*? Or does it feel a bit jarring and sad? "When anything by [Nirvana] comes on the radio, you almost have to pull over—still," says Seattle-based producer and former Fastbacks guitarist Kurt Bloch. "Since he's not around anymore, the music becomes a stronger reminder of that time."

Nirvana may sound somewhat like today's modern-rock playlist, but their music *feels* very strange. The songs elicit perplexing emotions. For one thing, it's hard to headbang to a saint.

And this guy's image pushes some hard-wired buttons. I mean, look at him. The striking clear-blue eyes. The sharp, nobly set features. The thousand-yard smirk coming out of the photos and videos. The unkemptness almost makes him more dusty-prophet biblical. And listen to the oblique, electrifying lyrics and airy vocal lines, the way they waft on surprising harmonies over a neo-heavy-metal roar, leaving melodic vapor trails. In a way, the cynicism you feel you *should* have about all the grunge mythologizing smacks of a naysayer's denial.

Then there's the story. The book of Saint Kurt has it as follows: Our sad, sensitive little Pisces-Jesus man is born in the wilderness of Washington, grows up among the heavy-metal heathens, hears the gospel of punk rock, forms a trio to make a joyful noise, is seized by the hypocrites, forced into superstardom, and martyred. "Their music became popular at a time when everything else sounded so stale and manufactured," says Jonathan Poneman, cofounder of Sub Pop "Nirvana always sounded pure—even at their most compromised, which by most others' standards wasn't compromised at all."

Because of this, many have attributed an almost divine purity to Cobain himself. And after the ensuing decade of chest-waxing Vedder clones and bling-blinging *Cribs* goons, he looks downright otherworldly. He couldn't have swum in the same crass, commercial water as the rest of us, could he? Goldberg, for one, says yes. "He didn't like all the consequences of fame, but he chose to come to Los Angeles and to sign with a major label. Other artists haven't done that. Fugazi didn't do that Superchunk, Pavement—all sorts of artists didn't do that. He was going for it; he didn't only write the songs, he designed the T-shirts, he wrote the scripts for the videos, he rewrote the bio."

Consider "Smells Like Teen Spirit," the song that just *happened* to rock the reigning order like a force of nature. But look at the journals—there, Cobain's description of the video reads more like a giddy cultural campaign: "The first one, 'Smells Like Teen Spirit,' will have us walking through a mall throwing thousands of dollars into the air as mallgoers scramble like vulchers [*sic*] to collect as much as they can get their hands on, then we walk into a jewelry store and smash it up in anti-materialist fueled punk rock violence. Then we go to a pep assembly at a high school and the cheerleaders have anarchy A's on their sweaters and the custodian-militant-revolutionarys [*sic*] hand out guns with flowers in the barrels to all the cheering students who file down to the center court and throw their money and jewelry and Andrew Dice Clay tapes into a big pile, then we set it on fire and run out of the building screaming. Oh, didn't Twisted Sister already do this?"

Cobain's journals are filled with his analysis of the waning generation gap, a sense of the rebellious possibilities in his peers; and a real concern for how he fit in with people his age. Unlike, say, Jack White, who has one foot in some gothic Delta/Nashville past, Cobain was fixed in the here and now, maybe fatally. "He sometimes hated himself for wanting [stardom]," says Goldberg. "He was a complicated guy, and there are things that you don't always know you're getting into. But he became a rock star on purpose. He *hired* me to do that. No one put a gun to his head. He put his own gun to his head."

This is an older part of the ghost story. You may want to be rich and famous, you may want your music to reach millions, but you don't want to be Generational Spokesperson. It's like, if you're in a Greek myth, you don't want to be the *most beautiful* heroine or the *mightiest* warrior. Pretty damn beautiful or mighty freakin' strong is fine. But not the most. That's the one the gods fuck with, the one they enlist as a plot device for wars and mass murders. Odysseus or Eddie Vedder might turn out okay. But Achilles? Kurt Cobain? No thanks.

In the headline of its front-page obituary, *The New York Times* bestowed on Kurt Cobain the absurd title "Hesitant Poet of 'Grunge Rock.'" Sociologically, the term "grunge" echoes "punk"—another vague, contested, commercialized catchall applied by various segments of society to a huge array of ideas, sounds, styles, and personalities. It's ridiculously imprecise and inadequate, but that's the unholy deal you cut when you want to make a big noise in the world. You detonate the explosion, change things forever, and the meanings scatter.

A whole generation of musicians was picking through such scattered meanings in the long march from "punk" to "indie" to "alternative"—before Nirvana came to represent the entire decade-plus tradition in the mainstream. From adamantly underground bands like Black Flag, Minor Threat, the Minutemen, and Big Black to major-label signees like the Replacements and Dinosaur Jr. to countless other arty or freaky institutions, the music scene was very much the "little group" suggested in "Smells Like Teen Spirit." It was a complex, long-percolating mixture to so suddenly spurt up in a single super Venti cup of Seattle sludge.

But what about now? Has Nirvana's legacy—their irrational rock exuberance—been purged? Or worse? Have we returned to the George Bush/Michael Jackson administration of 1990—only in a newer, creepier version? As we speak, Nirvana's moment is being packaged for your nostalgic enjoyment, in something that sounds like a late-'90s *Saturday Night Live* skit: "alternative gold," a paradoxical new radio format pioneered by KBZT in San Diego that plays all your favorite grunge hits. It could be an update of the infamous ad for a classic-rock compilation that aired in the mid-'80s. Two hippie dudes sit outside a van as their boom box blasts the opening riff of "Layla." "Hey, is that Freedom Rock, man?" asks one guy, perking up from his private purple haze. "Yeah, man," replies the other. "Well, *tuuuuurn it up*!"

Of course, parts of Cobain's spirit—the violent, the gentle, the weird—are alive in pop music. Is Eminem, for instance, carrying some mystic Cobain gene? Both have alter egos: Kurdt Kobain, Slim Shady. Both were (are) left-handed, mom-hating, daughter-having, dysfunctional-wife-marrying, grossness-loving, rhyme-spitting little guys who were utterly remade by a musical subculture, then tried to represent it as subverting the mainstream—even when it became the mainstream.

But obviously, there's a huge gap between a gay-baiting rapper who "just don't give a fuck" and Kurt Cobain. To write songs like Cobain's, you need more than imagination, verbal dexterity, and a gift for dynamics and melody. You sort of *have* to give a fuck—about people different from yourself, about problems beyond your experience. "Kurt was really into expressing an allegiance to sensitivity as opposed to [being] Mr. Tough Guy," recalls Moore. "You see kids into the whole Cobain thing [now] who are outcasts from the rap-metal, baseball-hat-wearing Limp Bizkit kids, the middle-class teenage gangstas. It would have been interesting to see how Kurt would've reacted to all that."

Cobain certainly didn't seem thrilled with humanity; it's safe to say he was a snob. But his ability to connect with other viewpoints was almost reflexive. For every lyric that sounds like a piss rant about fame, there's one like "Polly," based on a news story of a rape/murder, that shows a scary level of empathy for both victim and killer. Ruminating in the numb cadence of the killer's thoughts, Cobain nods forward to a conclusion that indicts the dark side in everyone. It's the song Bob Dylan reportedly singled out at a Nirvana concert, saying, "The kid has heart."

So many musical styles exploded throughout the '90s with their genre-hopping, crowd-surfing partisans. But something about the Nirvana ethos spoke to a larger truth about growing up in a particular post–baby boom world. It was ironic, sure, but also vulnerable, self-effacing, conscientious, trying hard to be cool, but not "cool." Come as you are—unless you're a jerk. Even the idea of coolness was associated with an underdog conscience, if only as a reaction to the regressive Republican, hair-metal social order it came up under. Sure, the shortcomings were easy to caricature. Cobain's end briefly stamped a whole scene and cultural experience—if not a generation—with the reputation of being amoral, sarcastic, solipsistic, self-pitying drama queens. Rock triumphalists from Gene Simmons to Noel Gallagher made a point of denouncing the brooding crybabies of '90s rock, as if Nirvana had ridden to massive pop-music fame on a staunch anti-fun platform.

Megan Jasper, then Sub Pop's receptionist, now the label's general manager, demurs: "They were really, really funny, goofy guys. They'd really 'blow into town'—it was sort of an event. I remember them showing up at the office on mornings after shows, all hungover with makeup running down their faces." Moore, too, had a different sense of what the pre-MTV mosh pit meant. "Punk-rock culture was very celebratory. Anybody who was involved with it was just having the best time of their lives. The nihilism and negativity were sort of elemental tools for attacking boredom, just an affront to conservative standards."

But people are always uncomfortable with something as mainstream as Nirvana that doesn't make its meanings clear or its intentions obvious. Everybody knows how to react to a Super Bowl "wardrobe malfunction"—with outrage, delight, or indifference, depending on your own little group. But a dress-wearing, golden-boy, junkie, rock-cliché, rock-original, underground superstar whose lyrics mixed jokey word games with agonized confessions and self-destructive tirades? He was always going to be problematic. Even for the little group that raised him.

As Cobain wrote in *Journals*, "I like to be passionate and sincere, but I also like to have fun and act like a dork." There's something noble about that honesty and about the attempt to embody both those personalities, maybe even something "American" in the best sense of the expression. But this too had its consequences.

An Egyptian papyrus scroll bears what some believe is the first-known suicide note. It begins "Lo, my name is abhorred / Lo, more than the odour of carrion / On summer days when the sky is hot . . . Death is before me today / As the odour of lotus flowers / As when one sitteth on the shore of drunkenness." If they'd had irony back in ancient Egypt, the author might've just written "I hate myself and want to die" and jumped in the Nile.

The irony, apathy, and general ennui that pundits attributed to Kurt Cobain's age group was supposedly a reaction to the sense that everything had been tried, every rebellion co-opted, every truth a cliché. So it's doubly ironic—if such a thing is possible—that fans growing up now think of Cobain as a valiant symbol of a time when rock music was more real and meaningful. But they do, and they're not entirely wrong. No one knew what was going to happen when Nirvana began their assault on history and culture (and MTV). Cobain had to traverse the '90s along with the rest of us. And as someone who is exactly his age, I can assure you that he wasn't the only casualty.

No "poet of grunge rock" could have been a devout practitioner of Shinto, whose central tenet is physical cleanliness. But Cobain's tale fits eerily well into that world of larger, older stories.

For instance, Siddhartha Gotama was his own form of anemic royalty, when, at the age of 29, he left his home, family, and title to find an answer to human suffering. He renounced the world he knew, fasted, searched, attained wisdom, and reached nirvana. He became known as the Buddha, the supremely enlightened being. Kurt Cobain addressed his suicide note to an imaginary childhood friend, someone he'd often talk to as a young, haunted boy. The friend's name was Boddah.

But this isn't religion we're talking about, it's pop culture: prepackaged, market-tested, owned, and directed by massive corporations that exploit the desires and neuroses of a young and impressionable public. Still, memory lingers, just like the word itself in the chorus of "Come as You Are." And, that ghost is out there. Whether it's sad, pissed-off, or exuberant, it's not going away until we do. One of the best aspects of punk rock, at least the American version Kurt Cobain grew up with, was the power of its audience—the scene, the community. Japanese religious experts say it's very difficult for a foreigner to embrace Shintoism: unlike most other religions, there is no one book that will teach a person how to practice the faith. It's transmitted from generation to generation, as people experience the rituals together. Which is what we're still doing, you and I, right now.

Additional reporting by Hannah Levin

EDITORS OF *THE ONION*

Heartbreaking Country Ballad Paralyzes Trucking Industry

NASHVILLE, TN—The interstate trucking industry, already beset with rising fuel prices and a shortage of qualified workers, was dealt another blow last month, with the release of the agonizingly sorrowful country ballad "She's Gone Back To What She Calls Home," by Cole Hardin.

"At any given time, day or night, an estimated 45 percent of the nation's over-the-road truckers are idling on the shoulder, in waysides, or in truck-stop parking lots, listening to Mr. Hardin's ballad of infidelity, loss, and heartbreak," said Russell Knutson, a spokesman for trucking giant Schneider National. "There's been an alarming number of loads that don't make it to their destination. And the ones that do make it are usually behind schedule, because they're being loaded, transported, and unloaded by crews brought low by the thought of a good-loving woman a man loves best packing everything up but her wedding dress and going back to the town she never should've left."

"'Scuse me a moment," Knutson said. "Sorry, but I must've gotten something in my eye just then."

Performance figures for the entire North American continent have suffered since the May 14 radio release of the "She's Gone

Back" single, from the album *Fenced In Heart.* Last week, the Department of Transportation reported business volume down 60 percent, manifest damage up 9 percent, and worker productivity down across the board, as drivers complain of heartache, loneliness, and the she-ain't-never-comin'-back-again blues.

"This isn't an easy job, no sir," said Arrow Trucking Company driver Wayne Crudup, 33, of Lexington, KY. "Long hours, tougher regulations every year, and lots less money than you'd like. Now, on top of that, I can't stop thinking of how that lady left that little home and that poor guy all alone, all because his eye went wanderin' where it never shoulda been. The song starts going round and round in your head, and it gets a touch hard to see the road sometimes."

National Surface Transportation Board statistics have shown a clear link between the playing of "She's Gone Back" on public airwaves and lulls in the trucking industry. The effects are especially noticeable in the South and Midwest.

"Unfortunately, country-radio stations nationwide have 'She's Gone Back' in heavy rotation," NSTB spokesman Howard Stivoric said. "The steel guitar's wail invokes the cold, hard, lonely road she's taking back to where her heart'll stop breaking, and, well, that makes anyone who hears it want to turn right around and get on back to where they came from. For a country that transports 85 percent of its perishable goods by truck, a heartbreaking ballad like this one is bad news."

Due to the song's popularity, the average trucker is spending as many as three hours per day sitting motionless in the breakdown lane. Travelers on the nation's highways are growing accustomed to seeing dozens of semis pull over to the side of the road whenever the song is played.

"We're especially worried about routes through trucking's Golden Triangle: Atlanta, Memphis, and Nashville," National Highway Traffic Safety administrator Dr. Jeff Runge said. "The high volume of country stations in that area, many of which confess to playing the song almost hourly, has created a depression hot-spot. Almost nothing's getting into or out of that area."

Fearing for the financial and emotional safety of their workers, industry leaders have asked President Bush and the FCC to remove the song from the airwaves, as President Carter did during the "He Stopped Loving Her Today" crisis of 1980.

Hardin, the singer responsible for the problem, was unavailable for comment, as he is currently in his hometown of Green Hills, SC, caring for his dying mother and writing "She Taught Me How To Love," a tribute to her 46 years of service as a devoted wife and parent.

ANN POWERS

Edelweiss

NOTE: THIS APPEARED AS PART OF A SERIES CALLED "BOOKMARKS," PUBLISHED BY SEATTLE RESEARCH INSTITUTE—TINY "BOOKS" IN THE FORM OF BOOKMARKS SOLD IN LOCAL AREA BOOKSTORES.

Everybody knows that the flow of life constitutes a great forgetting. It's worse than you think, though. Let's consider what we have let go, what's let go of us. We trust that it's the stupid stuff. What I had for dinner on the third Wednesday in January 1994. The name of the girl you flirted with the afternoon before you met your future wife. Yet my tuna casserole and your random encounter, Clarissa, linger on, stains on the mental carpet. And your wife, Joelle, turns to you and says, honey, I can still remember how it felt the first time we made love, on those faded gray poly-blend sheets in your rooming house on Fulton Street. You smile, of course, yes, your expression a memoir of her scent, your moans, the dawn light. Except really it's all a blue-red blur, not anything like the dyed-black pixie hair and slightly sweat-pungent green T-shirt dress of Clarissa.

The mind is kind, though, and such momentous lapses occur unbeknownst even to yourself. The blue-red blur satisfies. Soon enough, the fiction you offer others becomes your own reality. Our history is what we tell ourselves, until disaster strikes. That's why, to confront the genuinely frayed relationship each of us has to our own histories, it's much more useful to start with a song. You can't fake someone else's lyric—it's in there, like a prayer, or it's gone. The lyric or melody forgotten is like a termite spotted on your brain's basement floor, its tiny presence signaling the rot within the identity you've lovingly constructed. Sure, wear the T-shirt you bought to wear on the crazy weekend you spent following Pearl Jam down the coast in 1995. But tell me, what is the third line of the second verse of "Why Go Home"? Didn't you yell it out from the third row night after night? Now it's disintegrated, taking with it the sense you've so proudly made of your past.

Here's how something similar happened to me one night not so long ago. Three twenty-four a.m., said the digital readout. My baby daughter's time. She is raw in the world, too turned around to know day from night, and at the moment she needed succor. After food and gentle squeezing, that meant music. I sleepily thrilled at the opportunity to swaddle her in my soundtrack. Where to start? My favorite songs, of course.

Now, I should pause for a moment and tell you why songs shape my brain more than they might shape others. It all started when I was a lonely little misfit, a childhood condition I hope not to pass down, though it did allow me to cultivate a certain singularity. Having no schoolyard friends, born too soon for email buddies, I sought solace in the radio. Soon enough I graduated to my own record collection, and the saga continues: the songs spoke to me. I talked back. I became that type, the music lover. Other outcasts clung to pets, beginning their journey toward veterinary degrees, or hunched over chessboards on their way to the labs at Xerox and IBM. For me, the game board held record stores, music magazines, and a future in what corporate types call "the industry."

Music became my career, but on a more intimate level, it remained my diary. These are the revelations one makes to a daughter before she can talk: inherited secrets. So with my daughter in my arms, I quietly but eagerly began to sing. There would be no "Row Your Boat" for her, but instead, the majesty of

Leonard Cohen, the jazz of late-period Joni Mitchell, the sweet sorrow of Nick Drake. These were not anyone else's songs, as far as I was concerned. I offered them to her.

I started to sing that heavy-lidded morning, walking my little one into my consciousness. "Never knew magic crazy as this. . . . " But wait. What's the second verse of Nick Drake's lonely masterpiece? I tried again. "Here we are, stuck by this river. . . . " Brian Eno, where does your lyric flow? I took a break. It was late. At least I could do Bob Dylan. He was mine and everybody else's. But I lost the thread of "Just Like a Woman" after the part about amphetamine and pearls. Was the next verse time for me to quit? Or had I missed a bridge? Shaken, I turned to "Me and Bobby McGee," which was only sort of mine in that I liked it better than most songs beloved by millions. I got pretty far, but in the end lost the order of the melody. My tiny heir gazed up at me, happy just to feel the hum in my chest. But I was slowly feeling more and more crushed.

I turned on the television to tune out my failure. There on the screen danced Julie Andrews and those infernal Austrian children under her care in "The Sound of Music." Baby and I watched as they harmonized, tipping like teapots. The oldest one proceeded into puppy love. Maria married the Captain. Nazis menaced them. Escapes were planned. And then Christopher Plummer stood in the center of the screen, singing "Edelweiss."

The melody penetrated my ear like a parasite. "Every morning you greet me. . . . " Every word came back to me effortlessly. Suddenly I had no favorite songs, I had no memories at all, except what I had stumbled into utterly by chance. The notes in my head bobbed up and down, erasing the fiction I clung to with such pride, replacing it with a sort of jolly sense of pointlessness. It's not that I realized I was a different person than I'd imagined because I could croon a show tune. More that I suddenly knew I wasn't a person at all, at least not within a definition that included straight lines and neat boundaries. I, like you, am just a drawer full of circumstantial evidence, though I'm also the one given the job of making sense of the case.

And so I have been reminded of memory in all its cruelty: a real reflection of the tripping coincidence of days that add up to life, beyond legacy and the partial joke of free will. "Edelweiss," I sing to my daughter, every night now. I'm teaching her the process of becoming what she one day won't admit, and will never forget.

DAVID RITZ

The Last Days of Brother Ray

The sheer strength of his life force made me less afraid of death, but now that he is dead, now that our endless discussions about the nature of death are over, now that his own struggle with death is resolved, the question of death is more on my mind than ever. "Death," he said to me when he first learned that cancer was devouring his body, "is the one motherfucker that ain't ever going away."

I met Ray Charles in 1975, at a time in my life when I was haunted by the fear of death. This had been the case since I was a little boy. In college I had read the line by 17th century poet Andrew Marvell, "At my back I always hear Time's winged chariot hurrying near." I took Time to mean Death. To defy death meant to hurry into life. If I could convince Ray to let me write his life story in his own words, my own life would change. I could go from being an advertising copywriter to an author. The obstacles, though, were daunting. Ray was unrelentingly private. When not performing, his whereabouts were well-guarded secrets. His underlings were instructed to stop people like me from approaching him. What's more, I lacked the qualifications. I'd never written a book before.

But frantic determination was my ally. My future was in the balance. I had to find a way to get past his handlers. Salvation came in the form of Western Union. By sending him long telegrams in Braille, I reasoned rightly that no one but Ray could read them. The telegrams set out my impassioned argument: that I could capture his voice and translate the pulse of his music into musical prose. Ray bought the argument. We met, bonded and went to work.

The work of a ghostwriter is strange. Your job is to disappear and then reappear in the guise of another spirit. You lose yourself before finding yourself in someone else's skin. To do that you listen. You listen to the cadences, the stories, the beating heart beneath the stories. In listening, you pray for a mystical marriage between your soul and the soul of your collaborator. In listening to Ray, I was transported. I didn't merely like the way he spoke; I loved it. Early on I heard how the thrill of his music was even more thrilling in his speech. He was vulgar, refined, funny, sexy, spontaneous, outlandish, brave, brutal, tender, blue, ecstatic. He was wholly unpredictable. He wrapped his arms around his torso, hugging himself in a grand gesture of self-affirmation. To make a point, he beat his fist against his chest. His gesticulations, like his articulations, were wildly unrestrained. In normal conversation, he preached and howled and fell to the floor laughing. He had no trace of self-consciousness, no pretensions. He was, in his own words, "raw-ass country."

Because my job was to take the raw material of our dialogues and weave them into a first-person narrative, I had to make sure the dialogues were deep. I had to ask tough questions.

I began tentatively by saying, "Now if this question is too tough . . . "

"How the fuck can a question be too tough? The truth is the truth."

The truth—at least Ray's truth—came pouring out. That his life had been rough. That his life had been blessed. That he had followed his musical muse wherever it led. That he had been gutsy in traveling the long dark road, blind and alone. That he had been a junkie. That being a junkie never stopped him from working day and night, touring, recording, succeeding. That he had given up junk only when faced with prison. That every day he still drank lots of gin and smoked lots of pot and worked just as tirelessly. That he had a huge appetite for women. That he never curbed that appetite. That he wasn't even certain of how many children he had fathered. That he was unrepentant about it all. That he was more than confident; he was cocky; he knew his own powers—as a man, a musician, a lover, an entrepreneur who had outsmarted a ruthless industry, maintained ownership of his product and stashed away millions.

I'd never met anyone braver. He had no fears. He walked through the world like a lion. If anything, his handicap gave him an edge. His sightlessness intimidated adversaries. Rather than look *at* you, he looked *through* you. His mind was quicker than yours, his memory better, his instincts keener. Keeping up with him required resilience.

"We're flying out tomorrow," he said, a week into our interviewing.

My heart sank. I was deathly afraid of planes, especially small private planes like the one Ray was taking. But I said nothing. He was the star, I was the ghost. It was his book, not mine. My job was to catch him when I could.

Next day we ascended into an overcast sky. For the first hour, the little jet danced around the thunderstorms. Then darkness descended, thunder boomed, lightning flashed. We rocked from side to side; we dropped precipitously. Ray remained impervious. He was discussing his childhood. I was taping him and taking notes. The pilot opened the door to the cabin to tell us it would get even rougher. Ray didn't react. He couldn't have cared less. And suddenly I realized that, for all my years of fear, for all my paranoia about planes, I too was fearless.

As long as I'm with this man, I silently said, *God will dare not touch me. God will dare not touch me because God will dare not touch Ray.*

Ray doesn't fear God. If anything, God fears Ray.

The senselessness of my thoughts made perfect sense to me. The plane landed safely in Chicago, and that night, after the gig,

Ray and I were deep into a discussion about fear and faith, the Grim Reaper and the Almighty.

"When my mother died, I didn't understand death," he said. "Couldn't feature it. What do you mean she's gone forever? I was 15, living at a school for the blind 160 miles away from home. She was all I had in the world. No, she couldn't be dead. She'd be back tomorrow. Or the day after. Don't tell me about no death. Death can't take this woman. I need her. Can't make it without her.

"That's when I saw what everyone sees—you can't make a deal with death. No, sir. And you can't make a deal with God. Death is cold-blooded, and maybe God is too. So I'm alone, and I'm going crazy, until Ma Beck, a righteous Christian lady from the little country town where I grew up, wakes me and shakes me and says, 'Boy, stop feeling sorry for yourself. You gotta carry on.' "

I wondered if the experience made him more religious.

"Made me realize I had to depend on *me*," he shot back. "No one was going to do shit for me. You hear me? *No one*. I could praise Jesus till I'm blue in the face. I could fall on my knees and plead. Pray till the cows come home. But Mama ain't coming back. So if Mama gave me religion, the religion said, 'Believe in yourself.' "

"And not Jesus?" I ask.

"Jesus was Jewish, and if he couldn't convince his own people he was the messiah, why should I be convinced? I could believe in God. I was scared not to. And I sure as shit could believe in the devil. But I had problems with Jesus."

Early the next morning we flew on to New York. I was eager to continue the conversation.

"Ray, I just want to ask you another question about death . . . "

"Look, man," he said, irritated and tired, "I wouldn't talk to my mama now if she came out the grave." And with that, he fell asleep.

Most of our discussions took place in the recording studio in the back of the modest office building at 2107 West Washington

Boulevard he had built in 1964. He owned the place, in the shadow of downtown Los Angeles, outright. Because he had memorized the floor plan years before, he knew every inch. The moment he stepped inside, he was no longer blind. He ran up and down the halls like a kid. The studio was his playpen, the place where his fascination with machines and music forged into a permanent obsession. The studio was also where he exercised absolute control.

He routinely called me after he had been recording for several hours and was ready to wind down. That was usually the middle of the night. When I arrived, the first thing I noticed was the enormous key ring he carried with him. Keys to his house, cars, studio, cabinets, safe.

"Every key unlocks something I own," he explained. "Don't owe nobody nothing. Ain't afraid of nobody."

I wondered if his hard-earned wealth was one of the reasons he didn't seem to fear even God.

"Wrong," he said bluntly. "The thing about me, man, is that I never change. *Never*. Back in the fifties, when I was taking little gospel songs and turning them into rhythm-and-blues, I caught hell. Preachers calling me a dirty dog. Saying I'd rot in hell. Well, I didn't have no money then. I was broke as a motherfucker, but I was the same Ray then as now. I was going to do what I had to do. I wanted to change up the music. Wanted to make some bread. And if God was going to strike me down dead for perverting his spirit, so be it."

We talked about the church—the country church of his childhood—projecting the same spirit of his blues-based music.

"I loved the church," said Ray. "Loved the jump-up-and-down feeling in there. Loved the ladies hooting and hollering. Loved the tambourines. Loved the shuffles and the back beats. Loved every goddamn thing about it. The church is my base. Without church, there's no me. But that don't mean I believe everything the church says. Years later I had an experience that made me think about the church. You'll appreciate it because you're Jewish. A friend took me to a synagogue, and guess what?

No shouting. No tambourines. No amen corner. No red-hot music."

"I know," I said. "It's boring."

"Not to me. To me it was chilled out. Calm. I dug it."

Brother Ray: Ray Charles' Own Story came out in 1978. Ray liked the book because, as he said, "it's me—and I like me." Our friendship continued. He'd occasionally invite me to recording sessions and concerts. I'd hand him the books I'd written with people he knew—Marvin Gaye, Aretha Franklin, BB King, Jerry Wexler, Etta James, Little Jimmy Scott—and he'd listen to them on a machine given to him by Stevie Wonder. I'd watch a half-dozen different producers try to produce his music. Finally, though, no one could produce Ray but Ray. Just as no one could manage Ray but Ray. That he fell out of fashion with the record business meant little to him. He still toured the world, still made millions. He knew that his seminal influence on American culture was permanent, his place in history secure. His bravado never waned.

"I can still sing my ass off," he said. "Besides, even if I never earn another penny, I got enough money to survive World War III."

His bravado was momentarily undermined in the eighties when an inner-ear infection had him afraid of going deaf.

"Being blind is one thing," he told me. "But being blind *and* deaf is some Hellen Keller shit I can't fathom. No ears, no music, no Ray."

But the infection healed and, after donating money to organizations aiding the deaf, life went on.

"I'm a man of routine," he explained. "Don't like changes. Don't like surprises. Just let me keep doing what I'm doing. If I can play a concert, if I can cut a record, and if at the end of the day I can top it off with a nice piece of pussy, well, what else can a man want?"

When he turned sixty in 1990, I asked him if he had regrets.

"About what?"

"Paternity suits from women who claimed they had your babies, law suits from musicians who claim you owe them money . . . "

"Mother-fuck it," he spat. "I paid what was due. Fact is, no one's paid dues like me. If someone can prove I owe him, I'll pay. If they can't, I won't."

When he turned seventy in 2000, I asked him if he wanted to collaborate on a sequel to his autobiography.

"All the facts are in *Brother Ray*. What would we talk about?"

"We'd reflect."

"About what?"

"The changes you've been through since 1978."

"I don't see no changes, baby. I'm still me. Still kicking plenty ass."

He beat his chest with his fist, leaned back in his big chair and grinned like a Cheshire cat.

Then in the summer of 2003 everything changed.

I read an article in the paper saying he was having hip problems and was canceling his world tour. Ray never cancels tours. I knew something was deeply wrong.

When I called Ray to express concern, he didn't sound right. Usually focused, always ebullient, he was distracted and subdued.

"My liver's not right," he said. "I'm not putting out no press release, but I heard them use the word cancer."

I was stunned. Other people got cancer, not Ray. Meanwhile, his office kept telling the press it was his hip. He'd have surgery. He'd be back in no time.

A month later my phone rang shortly after midnight. Ray wasn't talking about cancer but rather the fact that we used the same doctor, Alan Weinberger, who had diagnosed the disease.

"Alan's a beautiful guy," said Ray. "He always has hope in his voice. He says chemotherapy can do a lot of good."

Ray's voice was different, softer, almost vulnerable.

"I'm thinking," he went on, "that we need to add some stuff to the book. But right now I'm tired. I'll call you when I can."

Another five or six weeks passed before he called.

"Chemo kicked my ass," he said. "Nearly did me in. I was at death's door. It wasn't pretty."

"I'm sorry. The pain must be . . . "

"It ain't just physical, man. It's mental. It has you thinking."

"About?"

"Everything."

I waited for an explanation but none came. I let the silence linger. I didn't know what to say. I knew what I wanted to ask—*How are you dealing with the prospect of death? How are you feeling about God?*—but I couldn't initiate that subject. Only he could, and he chose not to. I could only tell him that I loved him and would keep him in my thoughts.

My thoughts were confused. His office gave out reports that he'd soon be touring. He was to give a concert in New York. He was going to Europe. He was giving the impression that all was well. But every time we spoke, he sounded weaker. I knew he couldn't tour, yet understood that he, the most determined of men, wanted the word out that nothing or no one would stop him.

"Someone said," he told me a little later, "that if you picture yourself well, you get well. If you can conceive it, you achieve it. I'm focusing on the future. But I got to say, man, that the past keeps coming up."

"What part of the past?" I ask.

"Some of it is funny shit. Like this one time from the early days. I was fucking someone's old lady when Mr. Someone came home. I didn't even know there *was* a Mr. Someone. But there we were, screwing like rabbits, when we hear the door opening and she's whispering, 'Oh, my God, it's my husband.'

"'What husband?' I want to know.

"'The one who's crazy jealous and carries a razor.'

"So she hides my naked ass in the closet where I'm praying to God for the guy to leave in a hurry. Man, I'm shivering. If I cough, I'm dead. If he opens the closet to look for his hat, I'm dead. No *What I'd Say*, no *Georgia on My Mind*, no *I Can't Stop Loving You*, no Grammys, no career, no nothing. But God hears me. God delivers me. The man splits. I'm saved. Now am I supposed to believe that the Good Lord spared me so I could have me some hit records, make me some money and get me some more pussy? Well, that don't make sense because God sure didn't save Sam Cooke. Sam was fucking the wrong girl in the wrong place at the wrong time and he got shot dead. Why Sam and not me? Church folks said cause Sam traded in gospel for the devil's music. Well, I did the same. No, man, you got to believe that God works in mysterious ways. And you got to believe that I've been blessed. My life has been beautiful. I've gotten to go everywhere I've wanted to go. Got to do it all. So I shouldn't have any attitude. None at all. Just accept my blessings and say, 'Thank you.' "

I found the courage to say, "Sounds like you're trying to convince yourself."

"You mean I should be angry about getting sick?" Ray retorts.

"You're entitled to whatever feelings you're feeling."

"I'm feeling like I want more time. Something wrong with that?"

"Nothing."

"But there's no appealing. There's no making deals. God doesn't work that way."

"How does He work?" I asked.

"He worked through Ma Beck—that's for sure. After Mama died, she kept me from going crazy. She set me straight. I know that woman sure-enough saved me. Or maybe it was God who saved me. God working through Ma Beck."

"Ma Beck would say it was Jesus working through her."

"What do you know about Jesus? Jews have a thing about Jesus."

"Mable John has been talking to me about Jesus," I said. "Mable has church in her home."

Mable John, the great rhythm-and-blues artist for Motown and Stax/Volt, is a former lead Raelette and one of Ray's closest confidants. Now she is a minister.

"I need to call Mable," said Ray. "Need to see her."

"I saw Ray," Mable told me a few days later. "Went over there and sat with him."

"Was he receptive?" I asked.

"He listened. He let me pray. He loved that I prayed. He said, 'John, never stop praying for me.' We read the 23rd Psalm together. He knew it. He had it memorized. It's taken him awhile to get there, but he knows his own strength isn't enough."

"I'm getting stronger," he said the next time he called. "I can feel it."

"Great. Heard you talked to Mable."

"Man, I been talking to Mable for 40 years. For 40 years she's been trying to save my sorry ass."

"Any progress?"

"How about you?" he asked.

"I've been reading the bible."

"I got my Braille copy. Always keep it with me."

"What's it telling you?"

"When we were writing my book I remember telling you that I'm not really looking at Jesus, I'm looking at God. Well, I'm looking at it differently now."

"How so?"

"I think about stories. Songs are stories. And if you're going to write a good song, you're going to have praise a woman. That's the key. And if you're writing a book about God, you're going to have praise God. That's what Jesus did. Praised the Father. Taught us about praise."

"Wasn't the church of your childhood all about praise?"

"Hello!"

"So you're wanting to praise?"

"I used to think all that church praise, all that hooting and hollering, was overdone. Stop shouting. Be cool. Besides, if God is God, why does He need all this praise? Now I'm thinking it ain't God who needs the praise; it's *us* who need to do the praising. The praise makes us stronger. That's why I'm getting stronger."

"What's the source of the strength?"

"Used to think it was me."

"You always preached self-sufficiency. Wasn't that your mother's lesson?"

" 'Once I'm gone,' she said, 'you're alone. Nobody can help you but you.' If she had said, 'Once I'm gone, Ray, pray to God and you'll be delivered,' that wouldn't have worked. I'd be back in Georgia with a dog and a cane. She knew me. She knew the world. She knew I'd have to fight the fucking world and bend it my way. So I bent it my way. That made me feel strong as Samson. But now I see my strength has limits. I see my strength starting to sap away."

"That's a scary thought."

"I ain't afraid to admit it. Folks say, 'Ray, you got balls. When you were just a little scrawny-ass kid you caught the bus from Tampa to Seattle and somehow got over. You rode a bike. You drove a car. You put together a band when everyone said you'd go broke. You ain't scared of nothing.' Well, maybe I got caught up in hearing that. Maybe that made me proud. Maybe that got me thinking, 'I'm in control of this whole motherfucking operation—my music, my band, my life, my ladies.' But soon as you start thinking that way, brother, run for cover. Cause someone's about to kick your ass."

"Is God kicking your ass?"

"God's teaching me to depend on something I can't see. I've always seen ahead of myself—how to buy a car or buy a building, how to start a publishing company or a record label, how to make more bread this year than last. They call that foresight, don't they? Well, I've been blessed with foresight. Thank you,

Jesus. But now it ain't serving me. Now I need another kind of sight."

A part of me wanted to see him; a part of me didn't. I'd heard that he was frighteningly changed. "You'll be horrified," said one of his close associates. "You won't want to look."

But when Ray called and said I could come by the studio, I dropped everything and ran. For nearly 30 years, that had been our way. When he was ready to talk, nothing got in my way. I cherished every minute I spent with him.

He was seated where he loved to sit most—behind the control board, his fingers running up and down the switches of the elaborate recording console that anchored his musical life. He looked smaller, thinner, certainly diminished but far from defeated. I thought of the hundreds of hours I had spent in this room eliciting the thoughts of his secret heart. I thought of the hundreds of thousands of hours he had spent here—singing, writing, playing keyboards, rehearsing singers, musicians, mixing his songs, recording his voice. That voice, once an instrument of unprecedented power, was reduced to a whisper. I had to lean in to hear. The great sensuality that once emanated from deep inside his soul was missing. His robust frame had melted into the frail body of a sick old man. I felt alarmed by the transformation, but also intrigued, excited, grateful to be by his side.

He was thinking about other musicians, now gone.

"Did I mention Erroll Garner in my book?" he asked, referring to the great jazz pianist.

"Can't remember. I think so."

"I think I talked too much about my own playing. Too much about myself."

"That's the nature of autobiography."

"I never came up with that 'genius' tag. Someone else did. I don't like the genius business. It's not me. Erroll Garner was a genius. Art Tatum. Oscar Peterson. Charlie Parker. Artie Shaw. Dizzy was a genius—the way he wrote, the way he played. I'm a utility man. I can do a lot of little things well. But I learned it all from others. Piano from Nat Cole. Singing from Nat and Charles Brown. I copied."

"And then innovated."

"The innovation was copying. Good copying. Great copying. But I wouldn't put me up there with Bird and Diz."

"And when they say you invented soul music, you're going to argue?"

"Maybe I put together two things that hadn't been put together before, but, hell, give credit to the church singers—Archie Brownlee, Claude Jeter—and the bluesmen—Big Boy Crudup, Tampa Red—where I got it from. I got enough credit. Let people know that it didn't come from me. It came from before me. Way before me."

"And way before Big Boy and Tampa Red. Didn't they get it from someone else?"

"But they didn't get no money for it, and I did."

"And you regret that?"

"I love that, man," he said, his voice growing a bit more animated. "Be lying if I said I didn't. Got bread to leave behind. Bread for charities. Bread for my kids. But for every musician out there who's made a name, there's a dozen cats back in Jacksonville or Dallas twice as bad as them. They just never got known. Think of my own band. Everyone knows Fathead Newman and Hank Crawford. And rightly so. Fathead and Hank are beautiful. But no one remembers Donald Wilkerson or James Clay or Leroy Cooper or Marcus Belgrave or Johnny Coles or Clifford Solomon. These are cats up there with with Coltrane and Miles. Mention them, man. Don't let them be forgotten. They got me where I needed to go."

"What else do you want to mention?"

"That I hurt some musicians."

"How?"

"Being too much in a hurry. Too impatient. Looking for everything to be perfect. Lost my head. Said some nasty shit to guys who didn't deserve it. You know me, man. I'm always fucking with the drummers. If they don't get my time, I pitch a bitch.

Treat them bad. I feel like I hurt people. I know I hurt people. Well, tell them I'm not an asshole. Tell them I have feelings too. I can feel their feelings, man. Tell them I appreciate them. Tell them . . . just tell them Brother Ray loves them."

He started crying. I'd never seen him cry before. Not like this. I fought to keep my composure, but couldn't. He turned away and signaled me to leave.

"I'm getting stronger," he said when we spoke again. "Having a good day and feeling *a lot* stronger."

"I'm glad."

It wasn't the hallelujah Ray Charles voice we know and love, but I could feel him trying.

"So I'm reading the Bible and seeing how Jesus cured all these blind people. What do you take that to mean?"

"He could change things."

"You don't take it literally?"

"I love metaphors," I said. "Jesus used them all the time."

"So if I pray for healing, can a metaphor heal me?"

"Why not?"

"When I was a kid and went blind, never dawned on me to pray for sight. When I got to the school for the blind, lots of kids did just that. I'd hear them at night. 'Sweet Jesus, let me see.' I laughed at them. 'Waste of time,' I said. 'You fools better play the hand you were dealt.' So what's I did. But now I'm going to tell you something that'll surprise you. I'm changing. I'm praying for healing. I don't want to see. I just want to live. See anything wrong with that?"

"How can I argue with you? I'm praying with you."

"And expecting the miracle?"

"Your whole life's been a miracle."

"Hello! So it's gonna happen. It *is* happening. Mable was talking about it the other day. She came over here, walked right in, kissed me on the forehead and squeezed my hand. 'Ray, ' she said, 'I've seen folks a lot weaker than you get healed. You're a man with a strong will. God likes that. God can work with that.

Now you got to work with Him.' 'Mable,' I said, 'I'm working hard as I can.' "

"You've always worked hard."

"Strange part is that this work ain't hard. It's easy. It's about letting go of a whole lot of dumb shit. Not feeling afraid. Feeling calm. I tell you, man, I'm feeling like I felt when I was a little boy in church when all the ladies would come round and hug me and make me feel safe. Those ladies had no fear. What does the bible say? 'A perfect love casts out all fear.' You believe it?"

"I believe the part that says God is love. If God is alive and well inside us, we'll never die."

"Is that the Right Reverend Mable John talking, or is that you?"

I laughed and said, "I thought *you* were the Right Reverend."

"I'm getting there, baby. I truly am."

The last time I saw him we didn't speak. He could hardly speak at all. It was at the end of April, 2004, less than a year since he had been diagnosed. By then much had changed. His deterioration was dramatic. Although the mainstream press left him alone, one tabloid ran a ghastly picture of him on page one under the screaming headline, "Ray Charles Dying!" I hadn't been able to reach him for six or seven weeks. His people told me he was talking to no one. Minister Mable John said otherwise.

"I was there the other day," she told me. "He's still going to his building every day. He's still goes into his studio. He's maintaining his routine. Routine is Ray's life. He'll never give up his routine. So they set up a bed for him where he used to work. He has all the nurses he needs. He says he has all he needs to get through. And I believe him."

"Is he peaceful?" I asked.

"He's determined. He can't be any other way. He's determined to come outside today for the ceremony."

The outdoor ceremony was to commemorate Ray's beloved professional home, 2107 West Washington Boulevard, as an historical monument. Mable and I arrived early and sat on the front row. The afternoon sun was hot. The festivities began without Ray. Where was he? Politicians and movie stars—councilmen, the mayor, Clint Eastwood, Cicely Tyson—testified on Ray's behalf. The media came out in force. I was relieved to know that the utilitarian complex Ray designed would not be torn down for a strip mall. He had spent more hours here than anywhere. This was his refuge from the world, his work space, his musical lab, the hub of his entrepreneurial soul. The speeches droned on. We waited. We wondered. And then the door to his building opened.

Seated in a wheel chair, Ray appeared in a crisply-pressed pin-striped suit. We stood to applaud. He was in obvious pain. Slowly, carefully, he was lifted from the chair and brought to the podium where his long-time manager Joe Adams placed Ray's hand over the plaque. Then Joe brought the microphone to Ray's mouth. The sound of the singer's voice was slight, distorted, slurred. His words were barely audible. He thanked the city for the honor and then paused. It was clear that he had more to say. The pause was excruciating. I felt him struggling for energy, for a single stream of breath. Finally the breath came:

"I'm weak," he said, "but I'm getting stronger."

The news came six weeks later on June 10. Ray was gone. My reaction was immediate: I had to hear him sing. I put on his live versions of "Drown In My Tears" and "Tell the Truth." Those were the songs that bonded his heart to mine when I was still a boy. After a good long cry, I called Mable.

"I know he's all right," she said. "I know he's found his strength."

KELEFA SANNEH

The Rap Against Rockism

Bad news travels fast, and an embarrassing video travels even faster. By last Sunday morning, one of the Internet's most popular downloads was the hours-old 60-second .wmv file of Ashlee Simpson on "Saturday Night Live." As she and her band stood onstage, her own prerecorded vocals—from the wrong song—came blaring through the speakers, and it was too late to start mouthing the words. So she performed a now-infamous little jig, then skulked offstage, while the band (were a few members smirking?) played on. One of 2004's most popular new stars had been exposed as. . . .

As what, exactly? The online verdict came fast and harsh, the way online verdicts usually do. A typical post on her Web site bore the headline, "Ashlee you are a no talent fraud!" After that night, everyone knew that Jessica Simpson's telegenic sister was no rock 'n' roll hero—she wasn't even a rock 'n' roll also-ran. She was merely a lip-synching pop star.

Music critics have a word for this kind of verdict, this knee-jerk backlash against producer-powered idols who didn't spend years touring dive bars. Not a very elegant word, but a useful one. The word is "rockism," and among the small but extraordinarily pesky group of people who obsess over this stuff, rockism is a word meant to start fights. The rockism debate began in earnest in the early 1980's, but over the past few years it has heated up, and today, in certain impassioned circles, there is simply nothing worse than a rockist.

A rockist isn't just someone who loves rock 'n' roll, who goes on and on about Bruce Springsteen, who champions ragged-voiced singer-songwriters no one has ever heard of. A rockist is someone who reduces rock 'n' roll to a caricature, then uses that caricature as a weapon. Rockism means idolizing the authentic old legend (or underground hero) while mocking the latest pop star; lionizing punk while barely tolerating disco; loving the live show and hating the music video; extolling the growling performer while hating the lip-syncher.

Over the past decades, these tendencies have congealed into an ugly sort of common sense. Rock bands record classic albums, while pop stars create "guilty pleasure" singles. It's supposed to be self-evident: U2's entire oeuvre deserves respectful consideration, while a spookily seductive song by an R&B singer named Tweet can only be, in the smug words of a recent VH1 special, "awesomely bad."

Like rock 'n' roll itself, rockism is full of contradictions: it could mean loving the Strokes (a scruffy guitar band!) or hating them (image-conscious poseurs!) or ignoring them entirely (since everyone knows that music isn't as good as it used to be). But it almost certainly means disdaining not just Ms. Simpson but also Christina Aguilera and Usher and most of the rest of them, grousing about a pop landscape dominated by big-budget spectacles and high-concept photo shoots, reminiscing about a time when the charts were packed with people who had something to say, and meant it, even if that time never actually existed. If this sounds like you, then take a long look in the mirror: you might be a rockist.

Countless critics assail pop stars for not being rock 'n' roll enough, without stopping to wonder why that should be everybody's goal. Or they reward them disproportionately for making rock 'n' roll gestures. Writing in *The Chicago Sun-Times* this summer, Jim DeRogatis grudgingly praised [Avril] Lavigne as "a teen-pop phenom that discerning adult rock fans can actually admire without feeling (too) guilty," partly because Ms. Lavigne "plays a passable rhythm guitar" and "has a hand in writing" her songs.

Rockism isn't unrelated to older, more familiar prejudices—that's part of why it's so powerful, and so worth arguing about. The pop star, the disco diva, the lip-syncher, the "awesomely bad" hit maker: could it really be a coincidence that rockist complaints often pit straight white men against the rest of the world? Like the anti-disco backlash of 25 years ago, the current rockist consensus seems to reflect not just an idea of how music should be made but also an idea about who should be making it.

If you're interested in—O.K., mildly obsessed with—rockism, you can find traces of it just about everywhere. Notice how those tributes to "Women Who Rock" sneakily transform "rock" from a genre to a verb to a catch-all term of praise. Ever wonder why OutKast and the Roots and Mos Def and the Beastie Boys get taken so much more seriously than other rappers? Maybe because rockist critics love it when hip-hop acts impersonate rock 'n' roll bands. (A recent *Rolling Stone* review praised the Beastie Boys for scruffily resisting "the gold-plated phooey currently passing for gangsta.")

From punk-rock rags to handsomely illustrated journals, rockism permeates the way we think about music. This summer, the literary zine *The Believer* published a music issue devoted to almost nothing but indie-rock. Two weeks ago, in *The New York Times Book Review*, Sarah Vowell approvingly recalled Nirvana's rise: "a group with loud guitars and louder drums knocking the whimpering Mariah Carey off the top of the charts." Why did the changing of the guard sound so much like a sexual assault? And when did we all agree that Nirvana's neo-punk was more respectable than Ms. Carey's neo-disco?

Rockism is imperial: it claims the entire musical world as its own. Rock 'n' roll is the unmarked section in the record store, a vague pop-music category that swallows all the others. If you write about music, you're presumed to be a rock critic. There's a place in the Rock and Roll Hall of Fame for doo-wop groups and folk singers and disco queens and even rappers—just so long as they, y'know, rock.

Rockism just won't go away. The rockism debate began when British bands questioned whether the search for raw, guitar-driven authenticity wasn't part of rock 'n' roll's problem, instead of its solution; some new-wave bands emphasized synthesizers and drum machines and makeup and hairspray, instead. "Rockist" became for them a term of abuse, and the anti-rockists embraced the inclusive possibilities of a once-derided term: pop. Americans found other terms, but "rockist" seems the best way to describe the ugly anti-disco backlash of the late 1970's, which culminated in a full-blown anti-disco rally and the burning of thousands of disco records at Comiskey Park in Chicago in 1979: the Boston Tea Party of rockism.

That was a quarter of a century and many genres ago. By the 1990's, the American musical landscape was no longer a battleground between Nirvana and Mariah (if indeed it ever was); it was a fractured, hyper-vivid fantasy of teen-pop stars and R&B pillow-talkers and arena-filling country singers and, above all, rappers. Rock 'n' roll was just one more genre alongside the rest.

Yet many critics failed to notice. Rock 'n' roll doesn't rule the world anymore, but lots of writers still act as if it does. The rules, even today, are: concentrate on making albums, not singles; portray yourself as a rebellious individualist, not an industry pro; give listeners the uncomfortable truth, instead of pandering to their tastes. Overnight celebrities, one-hit-wonders and lip-synchers, step aside.

And just as the anti-disco partisans of a quarter-century ago railed against a bewildering new pop order (partly because disco was so closely associated with black culture and gay culture), current critics rail against a world hopelessly corrupted by hip-hop excess. Since before Sean Combs became Puff Daddy, we've been hearing that mainstream hip-hop was too flashy, too crass, too violent, too ridiculous, unlike those hard-working rock 'n' roll stars we used to have. (This, of course, is one of the most pernicious things about rockism: it finds a way to make rock 'n' roll seem boring.)

Much of the most energetic resistance to rockism can be found online, in blogs and on critic-infested sites like ilovemusic.com, where debates about rockism have become so common that the term itself is something of a running joke. When the editors of a blog called Rockcritics Daily noted that rockism was "all the rage again," they posted dozens of contradictory citations, proving that no one really agrees on what the term means. (By the time you read this article, a slew of indignant refutations and addenda will probably be available online.)

But as more than one online ranter has discovered, it's easier to complain about rockism than it is to get rid of it. You literally can't fight rockism, because the language of righteous struggle is the language of rockism itself. You can argue that the shape-shifting feminist hip-pop of Ms. Aguilera is every bit as radical as the punk rock of the 1970's (and it is), but then you haven't challenged any of the old rockist questions (starting with: who's more radical?), you've just scribbled in some new answers.

The challenge isn't merely to replace the old list of Great Rock Albums with a new list of Great Pop Songs—although that would, at the very least, be a nice change of pace. It's to find a way to think about a fluid musical world where it's impossible to separate classics from guilty pleasures. The challenge is to acknowledge that music videos and reality shows and glamorous layouts can be as interesting—and as influential—as an old-fashioned album.

In the end, the problem with rockism isn't that it's wrong: all critics are wrong sometimes, and some critics (now doesn't seem like the right time to name names) are wrong almost all the time. The problem with rockism is that it seems increasingly far removed from the way most people actually listen to music.

Are you really pondering the phony distinction between "great art" and a "guilty pleasure" when you're humming along to the radio? In an era when listeners routinely—and fearlessly—pick music by putting a 40-gig iPod on shuffle, surely we have more interesting things to worry about than that someone might be lip-synching on "Saturday Night Live" or that some rappers gild their phooey. Good critics are good listeners, and the problem with rockism is that it gets in the way of listening. If you're waiting for some song that conjures up soul or honesty or grit or rebellion, you might miss out on Ciara's ecstatic electro-pop, or Alan Jackson's sly country ballads, or Lloyd Banks's felonious purr.

Rockism makes it hard to hear the glorious, incoherent, corporate-financed, audience-tested mess that passes for popular music these days. To glorify only performers who write their own songs and play their own guitars is to ignore the marketplace that helps create the music we hear in the first place, with its checkbook-chasing superproducers, its audience-obsessed executives and its cred-hungry performers. To obsess over old-fashioned stand-alone geniuses is to forget that lots of the most memorable music is created despite multimillion-dollar deals and spur-of-the-moment collaborations and murky commercial forces. In fact, a lot of great music is created because of those things. And let's stop pretending that serious rock songs will last forever, as if anything could, and that shiny pop songs are inherently disposable, as if that were necessarily a bad thing. Van Morrison's "Into the Music" was released the same year as the Sugarhill Gang's "Rapper's Delight"; which do you hear more often?

That doesn't mean we should stop arguing about Ms. Simpson, or even that we should stop sharing the 60-second clip that may just be this year's best music video. But it does mean we should stop taking it for granted that music isn't as good as it used to be, and it means we should stop being shocked that the rock rules of the 1970's are no longer the law of the land. No doubt our current obsessions and comparisons will come to seem hopelessly blinkered as popular music mutates some more—listeners and critics alike can't do much more than struggle to keep up. But let's stop trying to hammer young stars into old categories. We have lots of new music to choose from—we deserve some new prejudices, too.

LUC SANTE

I Thought I Heard Buddy Bolden Say

The Union Sons Hall stood at 1319 Perdido Street, between Liberty and Franklin, in the area of New Orleans known in the late nineteenth and early twentieth centuries as Back o' Town, which was among other things the unofficial black prostitution district, as distinct from the official white one, Storyville, a few blocks away. The hall was built sometime after 1866, when several "free persons of color" formed the Union Sons Relief Organization of Louisiana and bought a double-lot parcel for its headquarters. The only known photograph of the place was taken in the 1930s, a decade or so after it had become the Greater St. Matthew Baptist Church, and by then it certainly looked like a church, although this being New Orleans it is not impossible that it always had a steeple and Gothic arched windows. Anyway, it was a church on Sunday mornings for much of its existence, originally leased to the First Lincoln Baptist Church for that purpose. On Saturday nights, meanwhile, it was rented for dances which lasted until early light, so that the deacons must have put in a hard few hours every week washing up spilled beer and airing out the joint before the pious came flocking. At night it was known as one of the rougher spots in a rough area. It was razed in the late 1950s, along with most of the immediate neighborhood, its site now lost somewhere under the vastness of the Louisiana State Office Building.[1]

It is remembered solely because of those dances, and primarily because some of them featured Buddy Bolden and his band. Jazz is too large and fluid a category of music to have had a single eureka moment of origin, let alone a sole inventor, but just about everybody agrees that no nameable person was more important to its creation than Buddy Bolden. He was a cornet player, born in 1877, and he got his first band together sometime around 1895. He was known for playing loud—stories of how far his horn could be heard sound like tall tales, but are so numerous there must be something to them—and for playing loose and rowdy. He was by all accounts the first major New Orleans musician to make a virtue of not being able to read a score. You can begin to get an idea of how distinctive his band was from looking at photographs. The traditional-style brass bands of the era wore military-style uniforms, complete with peaked caps, as their parade-band successors do to this day; the getups proclaim unison and discipline, even if the New Orleans version allowed for more latitude than was the rule among the oompah outfits active in every American village of the time. The orchestras—the term was then applied to non-marching musical agglomerations of virtually any size or composition—dressed in mufti, but their sedate poses attest to rigor and sobriety. The John Robichaux Orchestra may have had a big drum, as shown in an 1896 portrait, but its legendarily virtuosic members look as serious as divinity students, and by all accounts they played as sweetly.

Buddy Bolden's band, on the other hand, is clearly a *band*, in the sense in which we use the word today. In the only extant photograph, circa 1905, each member has chosen his own stance, with no attempt at homogenization. They all rode in on different trolleys, the picture says, but up on the stage they talk to each other as much as to the audience. Drummer Cornelius Tillman is unaccountably absent. Shy Jimmy Johnson disappears into his bull fiddle. B-flat clarinetist Frank Lewis sits gaunt and upright as a picket. Willie Warner holds his C-clarinet with the kind of delicacy you sometimes see in men with massive hands. Jefferson "Brock" Mumford, the guitarist, looks a bit like circa–1960

Muddy Waters and a bit like he just woke up fully dressed and out of sorts. Willie Cornish shows you his valve trombone as if you had challenged his possession of it. Buddy Bolden rests his weight on his left leg, holds his little horn balanced on one palm, shoulder slumping a bit, and allows a faint smile to take hold of his face. You could cut him out of the frame and set him down on the sidewalk outside the Three Deuces in 1944, alongside Bird and Diz, and then the smile and the posture would plainly say "reefer." You could cut him out of the frame and set him down on the sidewalk outside right now, and passing him you would think "significant character, and he knows it, too," and spend the rest of the day trying to attach a name to the face.

You can't hear the Bolden band, of course. They may actually have cut a cylinder recording around 1898, but the beeswax surfaces of the time were good for maybe a dozen plays, so it's hardly surprising that no copy has ever been found. And then Bolden suddenly and dramatically left the picture. In March, 1906, he began complaining of severe headaches, and one day, persuaded that his mother-in-law was trying to poison him, he hit her on the head with a water pitcher. It was the only time in his life that he made the newspapers. His behavior became more erratic, he lost control of his own band, and then he dropped out of that year's Labor Day parade in midroute—no small matter since the parade was an occasion for strutting that involved nearly every musician in the city.

Not long thereafter his family had him committed for dementia. His induction papers cite alcohol poisoning as the cause, but modern scholars suggest it might have been meningitis. In any case he remained incarcerated and incommunicado in the state Insane Asylum at Jackson until his death in 1931, aged fifty-four. He missed the leap of the New Orleans sound to Chicago and beyond, the rise of Louis Armstrong (who, born in 1901, may have remembered hearing Bolden play when he was five), the massive popularity of hot jazz that finally allowed acquaintances and quasi-contemporaries such as Freddie Keppard and Bunk Johnson to record, however fleetingly or belatedly. His name became known outside Louisiana only when white researchers from the North began knocking on doors in the late 1930s. He achieved worldwide fame as a ghost.

But let's get back to the Union Sons Hall. It's a Saturday night in July, 1902, and the temperature outside is in the lower nineties, with 83 percent humidity. The hall is typical for its place and function, an open room maybe twenty by fifty feet, made of white pine that hasn't seen a new coat of paint in a few decades, with no furniture besides a table for the ticket-taker and a series of long benches lining the walls, and no decor besides some old bits of half-shredded bunting tacked to the molding about ten feet up. There's a small raised stage at one end, with nothing on it but a few chairs and maybe Tillman's drums. People start trickling in around nine. They are local people, mostly single and mostly young, teamsters and plasterers and laundresses and stevedores and domestic servants and barbers and sailors and cooks. A few pimps and prostitutes are in the company as well, and a number of persons of no account, bearing names that may right then mean plenty in the neighborhood but will be preserved only as marginalia in the police records: Grand Jury, Cinderella, Pudding Man, Hit 'Em Quick, Ratty Kate, Lead Pencil, Two Rooms and a Kitchen. Someone may be selling glasses of beer from a keg in the corner, but many in attendance will have brought stronger sustenance in pint bottles. Within half an hour the room is already fetid with cigar smoke. As more and more people crowd in, the heat rises, and the air circulation slows to an ooze, and the air gradually becomes a solid, a wall composed of smoke and sweat and beer and rice powder and Florida water and bay rum and musk and farts.

By this time the band has been playing for a while. They have walked in through the crowd, carrying their instruments, jumped onstage and fallen to without fuss or fanfare. All of them are seated except Jones behind his bass, but they stand to take solos, and then the footlights reflected by tin disks make them look distended and not quite real. They have begun, per tradition, with the sugary stuff, "Sweet Adeline" and "A Bird in a Gilded Cage," maybe even given the nod to the sacred up front: "Go Down Moses," "Flee as a Bird." Maybe they've allowed some blues to trickle in, or proto-blues from the age-old fakebook: "Careless Love." To our ears they're playing these chestnuts pretty straight, with none of your cubist reconfiguration of the standards—that will come a couple of decades later, with Satchmo—but on the other hand the tunes are densely filigreed with embellishments and arabesques, and when Bolden plays you hear not so much the perfection of technique as the full range of the human voice. After a while they start to want to rag it, though, and Bolden calls out his transition number, "Don't Go Way Nobody," and then they throw down with "My Bucket's Got a Hole in It," which maybe Buddy wrote. By now they are as loud as if they stood in front of Marshall stacks, and the inside temperature is the kind to make cartoon thermometers balloon dangerously at the top, and the people on the floor are crazy, doing the Shimmy and the Ping Pong and the Grizzly Bear, shouting and stomping, losing sundry articles of clothing, in some cases dropping down cold along the wall.

But the band needs air. They need to fill their lungs to blow, remember? And the air is this yellow soup with filaments of monkey shit running around in it. So Bolden stands up, slices laterally with his hand, and the music stops, abruptly, right in the middle of the third chorus of "All the Whores Like the Way I Ride." Then he stomps hard once, twice, three times to get the crowd's attention. "For God's sake open up a window!" he bellows. "And take that funky butt away!" The crowd laughs. People look around to see who the goat is or to shift blame away from themselves, as somebody with a pole topped with a brass hook finally pivots open the tall windows. Everybody knows that this will mean noise complaints and then probably a police raid, but nobody leaves. Finally Bolden blows his signature call, and the machine starts up again. Afterward, people straggling home keep hooting, "Take that funky butt away!" For days they shout it in the streets when they're drunk, or they approach their friends very seriously, as if to convey something of grave significance, then let loose: "Take that funky butt away!" Various Chesters and Lesters in the area become "Funky Butt" for a week or a month, or for the rest of their natural lives. And then the hall, which everybody calls Kinney's after the head of the Union Sons, starts being referred to as Funky Butt Hall, and the name sticks.

Cut to a week later, to a dance at the Odd Fellows and Masonic Hall, a couple of blocks down on Perdido and South Rampart. In the second part of the set, right after "Mama's Got a Baby Called Tee-Na-Na," when everything is getting loose and crazy, Willie Cornish stands up and starts singing: "I thought I heard Buddy Bolden say / Funky butt, funky butt, take it away . . . " There is a silence from the crowd, and then pandemonium. People can't believe what they're hearing. It's as if the band had looked into their minds. And the song is more than a joke. It's a fully worked-out rag, immediately memorable on its own merits, while the words are irresistibly singable, a banner headline set to music. If there were records available, and people owned record players, storekeepers would not be able to keep copies on their shelves. Within a week or two dockworkers are singing it, and well-dressed young people are whistling it, and barbers are humming it, and drunks are caterwauling it. New verses proliferate. The tune, which instantly calls up the memory of the original words, is annexed by comedians and political campaigners and every sort of cabaret singer. Most of the versions are filthy, some are idle, some topical. For a long time the song goes unrecorded on paper, since even its title is unprintable, until an enterprising—not to say larcenous—ragtime publisher finally copyrights a wordless piano arrangement entitled, for some reason, "St. Louis Tickle."

For anyone who spent time at the dances and parades of black New Orleans at the very beginning of the century, though, the song will remain Bolden's monument, his living memory for decades after he is first locked up and then stone-cold dead, as the long line of graybeard interviewees of the earnest young Northern jazz fans knocking on doors from the 1930s to the

1960s will attest. Buddy Bolden wrote other songs, some of them—although attribution is always uncertain—more famous than he ever was, but "Funky Butt" is not merely his song; in alchemical fashion it has replaced the man himself. But no version of the lyrics was set down until an entire generation and then some had gone by.

Jelly Roll Morton, the Ancient Mariner of New Orleans jazz, finally recorded it three times in 1938 and 1939, once with the all-star New Orleans Jazzmen (including Sidney Bechet, Sidney de Paris, Albert Nicholas, Wellman Braud, and Zutty Singleton) and twice solo, accompanying himself on piano. The first of the solo recordings was made at the Library of Congress, where Morton spent three weeks reminiscing, orating, quoting, and singing for Alan Lomax's disc recorder, laying down songs and versions of songs so lavishly obscene they were not issued commercially until 1993. Morton copyrighted the song in his own name the next year, but for Lomax's recorder he paid tribute to Bolden—"the most powerful trumpet player I've ever heard, or ever was known."[2] This was around the same time that Bunk Johnson was alleging to William Russell and Stephen Smith that he had played with Bolden (he had to fiddle with the dates a bit to make his case), and five years after E. Belfield Spriggins published, in the *Louisiana Weekly*, the very first serious article on jazz ever printed in the state, in the course of which he gave Willie Cornish's version of the origin of "Funky Butt":

> It seems that one night while playing at Odd Fellows Hall, Perdido near Rampart, it became very hot and stuffy and a discussion among members of Bolden's band arose about the foul air. The next day William Cornish, the trombonist with the band, composed a "tune" to be played by the band. The real words are unprintable but these will answer: "I thought I heard Old Bolden say / Rotten gut, rotten gut / Take it away."[3]

Very little else has ever surfaced about the song or its origin. Russell and Smith's assertion that the number was "inspired by some 'low-life' women who had worked on a boat with the band"[4] sounds bizarre, and it was possibly concocted by Bunk Johnson. Morton remains the only person to have recorded the song who heard it played by Bolden's band. All three of his versions are consistent in lyrics and tempo—most contemporaries agree that they are far too slow. There are reminiscences galore of the song's scatological variant lyrics, but none ever seem to have been published, and Morton's version, in a series of recordings notable for probably containing the most uses of the word "fuck" previous to 1987 or so, is remarkably chaste. Besides the main verse, which is all most people know—funky butt, take it away, open up the window, let the bad air out—there is a second one in Morton's published version and on his second solo recording, about Judge Fogarty sentencing somebody to thirty days' sweeping out the market (a frequent punishment for minor infractions then) and something about Frankie Dusen (a trombone player who took over Bolden's band when he became incapacitated) demanding his money. Edmond "Doc" Souchon, a local musician, recalled a version from his childhood: "Ain't that man got a funny walk / Doin' the Ping Pong round Southern Park / Black man, white man, take him away / I thought I heard them say."[5] (The Ping Pong was a dance.) Bolden's biographer Donald Marquis suggests that the tune predated Bolden, that it was carried down the river, and he cites as corroboration words that do sound older than 1902:

> *I thought I heer'd Abe Lincoln shout,*
> *Rebels close down them plantations and let the niggers out.*
> *I'm positively sure I heer'd Mr. Lincoln shout.*
> *I thought I heer'd Mr. Lincoln say,*
> *Rebels close down them plantations and let all them niggers out.*
> *You gonna lose this war, git on your knees and pray,*
> *That's the words I heer'd Mr. Lincoln say.*[6]

Morton's recordings, for all their testamentary aspect and intent, can actually be seen as marking the start of a second life for at least one aspect of the song. Although *funk* is a versatile word, with secondary denotations of fear and depression and second-order thievery, the phrase *funky butt* would have clearly signified an odiferous posterior for at least a century before Bolden famously used the phrase, and in context it can still be so interpreted. In the glossary of hepcat jive that Mezz Mezzrow inserted at the end of his memoir, *Really the Blues* (1946), *funk* is defined as "stench," and *funky* as "smelly, obnoxious." In less than a decade, however, the meaning of the word had begun to turn, at least in jazz circles, particularly on the West Coast. The scat singer King Pleasure, backed by Quincy Jones, put out a record called *Funk Junction* in 1954, and 1957 saw the issue of *Creme de Funk* by Phil Woods and Gene Quill, and of *Funky* by Gene Ammons's All-Stars. In 1958 beatnik fellow-traveler John Clellon Holmes employed *funk* in a strictly musical sense in his novel *The Horn*, and not much later the word was being applied favorably to a performance by Miles Davis. By 1964 even the *New York Times* was throwing it around.

The word was in general currency from the early 1960s on as a musical term signifying some combination of authenticity, earthiness, greasiness, muscularity, perspiration, and the presence of one or more of the following: fuzz-tone bass, hoarse cries produced on the lower register of the tenor sax, a bottom-heavy and high-hat-intensive drum style, and a particularly dirty sound obtainable on the Hammond organ. The turning point came in 1966 when Arlester Christian wrote, and recorded with his band Dyke and the Blazers, the epochal "Funky Broadway," which was covered and made into a huge hit by Wilson Pickett the following year. The way *funky* was employed in the lyrics did not refer to music, although it retained many of the cluster of meanings associated with musical use: authenticity, earthiness, greasiness, etc. All of these dovetailed with and enlarged usefully upon the word's original olfactory denotation, welcoming the noxious odor and giving it a room and a new suit without actually rehabilitating it. From there it was a short step to Arthur Conley's "Funky Street" (1968), Rufus Thomas's "Funky Chicken"

(1970), Toots and the Maytals's "Funky Kingston" (1973), and "Funky Nassau" by the Beginning of the End (1973), among many. James Brown virtually bought the franchise, from "Funk Bomb" (1967) through "Ain't It Funky," "Make It Funky," "Funky Side of Town," "Funky President," "Funky Drummer," and scads more from all quadrants of meaning by a man who spent a year or two calling himself "Minister of the New New Super Heavy Funk." He had no peers atop the funk pyramid, or at least that was the case until George Clinton (of Funkadelic) concocted something like a theology of funk. (One of my proudest possessions is a T-shirt I can't fit into anymore that is emblazoned with the legend "Take Funk to Heaven in 77.") Clinton, in full evangelical feather, instituted a principle of spiritual surrender he termed "Giving up the Funk." This was *mana*, total communion with the life force manifested as a fried fish.

Funk has climbed down from those heights. It has been devalued by George Michael's "Too Funky," and the Eagles' "Funky New Year," and "Funky Funky Xmas" by the New Kids on the Block, not to speak of the lingering memory of Grand Funk Railroad. But the word has not been shucked. It is too valuable. It appears in hiphop strictly as a place-marker (the Notorious B.I.G.'s "Machine Gun Funk," Too Short's "Short but Funky," OutKast's "Funky Ride," etc.), but it is a place-marker that will not go away anytime soon. Payments are kept up on the word. Its license is renewed. It is periodically removed from the shelf and dusted off and cradled, occasionally taken for a spin to shake out the knots. The day will come before very long when it is immediately necessary once again, when all of its putative substitutes have been tarnished and made risible, when "ghetto" has been redeveloped and "real" become irredeemably fake—when it will have acquired a previously undreamed-of nuance temporarily undetectable by the white middle-class ear. It awaits a further development of the process set in motion on the rickety stage of some fraternal hall in uptown New Orleans in the year 1902 or there-abouts. It permanently embodies the voice of Buddy Bolden, speaking through a cloud.

Notes

1. This piece draws heavily on Donald M. Marquis's *In Search of Buddy Bolden, First Man of Jazz* (Baton Rouge: Louisiana State University Press, 1978; New York: Da Capo, 1980), a heroic piece of historical detective work that represents pretty nearly the last word on Bolden, who nevertheless remains a specter about whom more stories can be refuted than proven. Mention should also be made of the website maintained by Carlos "Froggy" May—www.geocities.com/BourbonStreet/5135/Bolden.html—which has stayed abreast of more recent scholarship, faint trickle though it is.

2. *Anamule Dance*, volume two of *Jelly Roll Morton: The Library of Congress Recordings*, Rounder Records 1092. Also see Alan Lomax, *Mister Jelly Roll* (New York: Grove Press, 1950).

3. E. Belfield Spriggins, "Excavating Local Jazz," *Louisiana Weekly*, April 22, 1933, p. 5. Quoted by Marquis, who sadly notes that "in 1965 Hurricane Betsy struck [Spriggins's] house and totally destroyed all the notes and records of his very early jazz research. His wife reports that he has been in such a serious state of depression since that he will not or cannot speak to anyone including herself" (Marquis, p. 109).

4. In *Jazzmen*, edited by Frederick Ramsay Jr. and Charles Edward Smith (New York: Harcourt Brace, 1939; New York: Limelight Editions, 1985), p. 13.

5. *Jazz Review*, May 1960.

6. Marquis, pp. 109–110, quoting Danny Barker, "Memory of King Bolden," *Evergreen Review*, March 1965, pp. 67–74.

DAVID SEGAL

The Shortwave and the Calling

In a cluttered home office in the World's End section of London, Akin Fernandez is trolling the dial of his newly acquired shortwave radio. It's December 1992 and it's late at night, when the city is quiet and the mad-scientist squawks of international broadcasts have an otherworldly tone. Fernandez, the owner and sole employee of an indie music label, is about to trip across a mystery that will take over his life.

Shortwave signals are bouncing, as they always do, around the globe, caroming off a layer of the atmosphere a few hundred miles above the Earth and into antennas all over the world. Fernandez can hear news from Egypt and weather reports from China. But his browsing stops when he tunes in something startling: the mechanized voice of a man, reading out numbers. No context, no comment, no station identification. Nothing but numbers, over and over, for minutes on end. Then the signals disappear, as if somebody pulled the plug in the studio. And it's not just one station. The more he listens, the more number monologues he hears.

"Five four zero," goes a typical broadcast, this time in the soulless voice of a woman with a British accent. "Zero nine zero. One four. Zero nine zero one four."

Numbers in Spanish, in German, Russian, Czech; some voices male, others female. When Fernandez lucks into hearing the start of a broadcast, he's treated to the sound of electronic beeps, or a few bars of calliope music, or words like "message message message." Then come the numbers. A few stations spring to life the same time each night, others pop up at random and cannot be found again.

At first, Fernandez figures it's a prank, the work of radio pirates with a sense of humor. But you need a license for this part of the radio band, and why would anyone break the law just to read digits into the dark yonder? In England the penalties are serious. Where's the comedic payoff?

Nobody has answers. Not the guy who sold him the radio, who claims they're weather stations—which is crazy, because weather stations don't hopscotch to different spots on the dial, as many of these did. Not a manual he buys about shortwave frequencies, which has a chapter on "numbers stations" and describes them as a riddle that nobody has solved. Not the British Library, which seems to have catalogued every other sound on the planet.

What's with the numbers?

Answering that question, it turns out, would take Fernandez years, and it left him nearly penniless, at least for a while. It also brought him a horde of admirers on another continent, eventually earned him a credit in a Tom Cruise movie and sparked a legal battle with the acclaimed band Wilco.

Fernandez would study numbers stations largely because he couldn't stop even if he tried—which is to say, he fell into the grip of an obsession. But along the way, by both accident and design, he discovered amid all that static the raw material for a point he likes to make, with characteristic zeal, about the future of rock-and-roll.

That, however, is later. In December of '92, Fernandez is just listening. And listening. He stays up till 4 or 5 every morning, jotting down frequencies and figures, looking for patterns. He keeps a detailed log, not for weeks or months but for years, without a clue about what exactly he is logging. Sometimes Fernandez doesn't leave his house for a week.

"You just get submerged," he says, on the phone from London. "You get immersed in it. There are so many questions and the only answer is to listen more, because no answers are coming from anywhere else."

The Secret Sounds

A few things you should probably know about Akin Fernandez: There's the basic background stuff—that he's the son of Nigerian-born parents, that he grew up in Brooklyn and moved to London when he was 15 years old. He calls himself a geek. He believes UFOs are real. More mysteriously, there appear to be grooves carved into his clean-shaven head, the origins of which he politely declines to discuss. ("Irrelevant," he says.) He is now 41. Also—and this is key—Fernandez hunts for audible thrills the way a shark hunts for meat, which is to say constantly and ravenously. This makes it a little easier to grasp his passion for numbers stations. They were unlike anything that had ever hit his ears.

And the radio counting wasn't just new to Fernandez, it was beautiful. He's a disciple of an Italian named Luigi Russolo, who argued in a 1913 manifesto called "The Art of Noises" that the bustle of city life and industrial machinery ought to be included in our musical language, alongside chords and harmonies, violins and oboes. This proved a tough sell. In 1914, Russolo held his first concert with noise-making machines he called Intoners and the show ended in a melee: performers against the audience.

"I understand that shortwave noise is a kind of music," Fernandez says, sounding Russolovian. "And to me the numbers brought another level of beauty to the music."

One final thing to know about Akin Fernandez: He's prone to fixations. His first was a collection of Marvel comic books that swelled to 5,000 when he was a kid. In his twenties, he noticed that literary-minded prostitutes in London were advertising their services, and phone numbers, with saucy little poems written on cards glued to the insides of phone booths. ("Once upon a time in Earl's Court / reigned the wicked Love Queen . . . ") For months, Fernandez would mortify friends and family by painstakingly peeling the cards off the glass, until he owned more than 600 of them. In 1984, he published the lot in a volume called "The X Directory."

"My mother came to the book party," Fernandez recalls. "I couldn't believe it."

Numbers stations, with their variety and quantity, triggered all of his impulses to catalogue and collect. The stations had personality, if you listened long enough. One always began with a few bars of "The Lincolnshire Poacher," an old British folk song. On another you could occasionally hear roosters or echoes of Radio Havana in the background, as though someone had forgotten to turn off a mike. One starred a young lady with an exotic accent who dramatically read words from the International Radio Operators alphabet, somehow making inscrutable phrases—"Sierra. Yankee. November."—sound life-and-death urgent.

While the rest of London slept, Fernandez chased these voices all over the dial, never sure when or where he'd find one. He wrote down the results in a green book bound with fake leather. A typical entry looked like this:

> Sept 6 '93
> Freq Time Signal
> 6.201 USB 12:30 am BIZARRE German Children's Voice
> Station starts with beeps, then
> GLOCKENSPIEL!! Then count
> From 1 to 10 then ACHTUNG!
> And message!! [expletive] Hell!!

There are a lot of exclamation points in Fernandez's log. "You're listening, and all of a sudden you come across a really strong signal," he says. "It's the most chilling thing you've ever heard in your life. These signals are going everywhere and they could be for anything. There's nothing like it."

To pay the rent, Fernandez released music through Irdial-Discs, which by then was part of a small ecosystem of clubs and record shops selling avant-garde music in London. Finally, after three years of wee-hours number logging, he heard about a book called "Intercepting Numbers Stations" by a guy named Langley Piece. He mail-ordered it from a place in Scotland, and when it arrived he sat and devoured it in a sitting. The book confirmed Fernandez's initial hunch—the stations were no joke.

"They're deadly serious, in fact," he says. "That little German girl reading numbers, she might be ordering someone to assassinate a person with a poisoned umbrella."

Mission: Indecipherable

Let's say you're a spy, out in the field, spying. You need instructions now and then from headquarters, but you don't want to risk exposure by picking up a phone (tappable) or getting an e-mail (traceable). Face-to-face meetings carry their own risks. What do you do?

One solution, dreamed up during the Cold War: Listen on shortwave radio at a predetermined time and frequency for a message that only you can understand. Numbers stations, it turns out, are the one-way chatter of espionage agencies to their spies. This isn't conspiracy theory hokum; it's referenced in a dozen-plus memoirs of assorted ex-spooks and defectors. And though numbers broadcasts might sound low-tech in the age of the BlackBerry, the idea isn't utterly cockamamie.

"In a two-way communication, you have to acknowledge the message," says David Kahn, author of "The Codebreakers," a history of cryptology. "But with a shortwave broadcast, anybody can listen, which means that nobody knows who the message is intended for."

The numbers, Kahn explained, are translated with the aid of what's known as a one-time pad, essentially a dictionary for a language that is spoken only once. Most pads are destroyed after a single use—some of the Soviet pads, lore has it, were edible—making them one of espionage's rarest artifacts. In 1988, three were found in a bar of hollowed-out soap when a Czech spy, posing as an art dealer in London, was caught by authorities as he sat in an apartment and transcribed a message sent via shortwave.

For Fernandez, this spy angle was a red rag to a bull. A dozen new questions arose, such as how much was all this costing tax-payers, and what messages were being sent? It irked him, too, that no government official, at least in Britain or the United States, would acknowledge this whole system was in place. He was unmoved by the argument that if the system were acknowledged it wouldn't be secret anymore. It didn't matter to him that the messages were totally indecipherable, or that nobody else seemed remotely worked up about them. The more Fernandez thought about it, the more outrageous it all seemed. British citizens—and citizens of other countries—underwriting secret messages, sent to agents, telling them to do God knows what.

"Even if you assume that most of the messages are 'pick up this money' or 'drop off the laundry,' think about what numbers stations represent. The only way a secret like this can be kept is if you live in a society where everybody is obeying and everybody is a little sleepy. But if you're a curious kind of chap you'll wonder, if your government can keep this a secret, what other secrets are they keeping."

If you knew Fernandez back in 1994, there was no talking him out of his numbers addiction. He claims he had a social life through his super-fixated years, but ask for the name of a buddy who knew what he was going through and he comes up empty.

Well, a girlfriend named Anne Marie came by one night and listened and her jaw dropped. More typical, though, was the reaction of a cousin who lives in London, who was perfectly baffled.

"I'd call and he'd say, 'I'm listening to something, do you want to hear it?'" remembers Enitan Abayomi. "And then I'd hear a voice over the radio. And I'd think, so? I just didn't hear what he heard in it. But he's very, very bright, and I often feel like he's leaving me miles behind. So I thought that people with higher IQs than mine might understand what he's talking about."

At some point, Fernandez began to think he'd never kick his numbers habit. It had pushed nearly everything else out of his life. He'd had enough, and in 1997, he tore himself, at last, from his radio. How did he do it?

"The Conet Project," he says.

The Leading Edge of Rock

In the annals of recorded music, you'd be hard-pressed to find anything rivaling the ambition and absurdity of "The Conet Project." (Conet, a word he heard often on the shortwave, is Czech for "end.") Four CDs with 150 different broadcast snippets from all over the world. More than 280 minutes of white noise, numbers and beeps. Plus a 74-page booklet with background, logs, playlists and a bibliography—the sort of treatment ordinarily reserved for platinum-selling bands with a massive fan base. Fernandez poured everything he had into "Conet." It sold in the United States for $62.

"I wanted it to be perfect," he says. "I didn't know what it would do, if it would just sit in boxes, because nobody had done anything like this before. But it was obvious to me that it had to be done."

This is a pretty succinct definition of obsession: a thing you feel you have to do, even though you don't, even if doing it will cost you everything, which is what it cost Fernandez. There were a few head-scratching reviews of "Conet" and sales of about 2,000 copies, modest even by indie standards. Fernandez closed up Irdial, and the last pressing of "Conet" was in 2001. He took a series of jobs that he'd rather not discuss.

"They were jobs," he says. "Just jobs."

That might have been it. But something happened. "Conet" slowly acquired a cult following. A fervent cluster of devotees cropped up in San Francisco, around a store called Aquarius

Records, a haven for the musical avant-garde, the sort of place that crows about albums such as "Insect Electronica from Southeast Asia." To Aquarius's owners and regular customers, "Conet" was a little ridiculous and totally irresistible. They posted a chart behind the cash register that tracked the store's "Conet" sales, and asked everyone who bought a copy to pose for a photo. They stopped with a photo of customer No. 386.

"It works in a lot of different ways," says Allan Horrocks, a co-owner of the store. "It's kind of creepy and mysterious because of what it is—this secret thing that you can't understand. We'd think it was cool if it was just an experimental drone record. But it's more than that."

Much more, actually. "Conet" gives off a whiff of the vaguely forbidden: Maybe the government doesn't want you to hear this. And your parents won't get it. And if you listen today, in the age of Code Orange, it actually sounds a little sinister, with echoes of the "chatter" the Bush administration is always warning us about. What could be more frightening than "chatter"?

"Conet," in other words, delivers a couple of the slightly subversive thrills that rock could once deliver without breaking a sweat. It feels new, a little dangerous, a ticket into a subculture of sorts. That's an experience you don't find in record stores much anymore, in part because rock has been around for 50 years—and can anything that old really feel dangerous?—and in part because corporate America long ago figured out there's gold in the underground, and now mines and mass-produces it faster every year. In a way, "Conet" is a measure of just how fringeward you need to head these days to find something that delivers the frisson of the margins.

Which is part of Fernandez's point. From the beginning, his label released what he calls "fine art noise" and "underground dance music," all of it made by a batch of artists you will never see on the charts. To Fernandez, Irdial's niche product occupies some of the only fertile ground left in music. It's his heartfelt belief that rock-and-roll has been dead for years. "Rock bands now are just following the path that's already been marked," he grumbles. "Right down to the riffs, right down to the production. These people are copying their fathers' record collections.

"I think the truly creative people have left this area. A real artist would look at the canvas and find the corner that hasn't been painted yet. Nobody is doing that. . . . The first thing that anyone in a band with a guitar and drums should do is put down their instruments."

So what's a rock band to do if it wants to keep the guitars and churn new ground? How do you make something so familiar seem daring?

Enter Wilco, a quintet that started as an alt-country act and is now boldly going where no rockers have gone before. Two years ago the group released an album with a song called "Poor Places." It starts as a droopy ballad, but eventually the drums fade, the melody evaporates, and up roars a truly terrifying hurricane of sound. As it builds to a climax, a woman's urgent semaphore peeks through the noise:

"Yankee. Hotel. Foxtrot. Yankee. Hotel. Foxtrot. Yankee. Hotel. Foxtrot." It's a track from "Conet," the voice of Ms. International Radio Operator herself. The band sampled it and used it to name the album. "Yankee Hotel Foxtrot" would earn Wilco its strongest reviews ever—it was No. 1 that year in the *Village Voice* national poll of music critics—and it sold decently, too.

At various moments on "Yankee" you can hear lead singer and co-songwriter Jeff Tweedy struggling with the where-do-we-go-now question. And he finds an answer, or at least part of an answer, in the same place as Fernandez, way way out there, in the ionosphere. Which is apparently where you wind up now when you seek the unpainted corner of the musical canvas.

It's enough to make you think that what's left of rock's frontier isn't very pretty; there isn't even music playing there. At some point—after punk crested, perhaps, in the late '70s—innovation in guitar pop became a matter of creative arithmetic. Blind Willie McTell plus Led Zeppelin times garage rock equals the White Stripes. The Velvet Underground plus the Cars divided by an intercom system equals the Strokes. But this has limits, too. The Strokes' second album, "Room on Fire," is just a rehash of their first. It's redundant and kind of gutless. It's everything that Fernandez hates. "Conet" ultimately defines the crux of rock's problem in middle age. How do you double back without seeming timid? How do you roll forward without seeming incomprehensible for its own sake?

On the Record

Though Fernandez and Wilco might sound like kindred spirits, they never exactly cozied up. The band didn't pay for that "Conet" loop, and in 2002 Fernandez sued.

For years, it's been Irdial's policy to post free downloadable versions of every song in its catalogue. (Head to Irdial.com to download any Irdial title, including the entirety of "Conet.") But Fernandez makes a distinction between personal and commercial use of his work. If you're going to make money from his labors, he thinks he should share in the wealth. At minimum, he thinks you should ask nicely. In 2001, he granted Hollywood director Cameron Crowe the right to several "Conet" cuts for use in the film "Vanilla Sky," free of charge, because Crowe requested permission. The cuts are heard in those arresting moments when Tom Cruise shows up in Times Square and discovers that he's all alone.

Wilco, the band's lawyers would eventually explain, figured there was no copyright on sound that anyone could have heard on the radio, that obviously wasn't a song and that hadn't in any way been artistically altered. Whatever the merits of the case—and Fernandez says the law in England is clearly on his side—Wilco settled out of court, saying it preferred to skip a drawn-out fight. That was in late June. The band's label sent Irdial-Discs, aka Akin Fernandez, about $30,000 to cover his legal costs, plus a royalty payment several times that sum. See if you can guess what Fernandez did with the money.

Today he is married, to Anne Marie, the one person who seemed to grasp the lunacy and charm of numbers stations, and they are raising four children.

Some family men might take a windfall like the Wilco loot and renovate the house, or take the kids on vacation. Fernandez didn't do that.

"The kind of guy who releases 'The Conet Project' isn't the kind of guy who goes on vacation," he says.

How about a new car?

"Absolutely not," he says.

Fernandez revived Irdial with the money, and he re-released "The Conet Project." New copies went on sale July 13 and the sales chart at Aquarius Records is back in action. In just a few weeks, the store has already sold 120 more copies.

"Conet," of course, will never earn a profit, but that was never the point. Fernandez calls it a total artistic triumph because it's in the Library of Congress, because it's in the British Library and because numbers stations are less of a mystery than when he first ran into them, 12 years ago. In 1998, a U.K. government spokesperson acknowledged for the first time that shortwave radio is indeed used for espionage.

"These [numbers stations] are what you suppose they are," the spokesperson told the *Daily Telegraph*, in a story that was prompted by the release of "Conet." "People shouldn't be mystified by them. They're not, shall we say, for public consumption."

To the untrained ear this might have sounded like an unremarkable brushoff. To Fernandez, it sounded a lot like "uncle."

NICOLE WHITE AND
EVELYN MCDONNELL

Police Secretly Watching Hip-Hop Artists

Miami and Miami Beach police are secretly watching and keeping dossiers on hip-hop celebrities like P. Diddy and DMX and their entourages when they come to South Florida, a move police say is to protect the stars and the public.

Officers say they have photographed rappers as they arrived at Miami International Airport. They stake out hotels, nightclubs and video shoots. They consult a six-inch-thick black binder of every rapper and member of his or her group with an arrest record in the state of New York. The binder begins with a photo and rap sheet of Grammy-nominated rapper 50 Cent. It ends with Ja Rule. Both men are embroiled in one of the most bitter feuds in the hip-hop industry, one that Eminem, 50 Cent's producer, has warned in the song Bully could lead to bloodshed. The policing effort of top entertainers—which hip-hop experts criticize as unnecessary stereotyping—was created, police say, to protect the public and musical celebrities who have chosen to make South Florida their destination to live and party.

"We have to keep an eye on these rivalries," said Assistant Miami Beach Police Chief Charles Press. "The last thing we need in this city is violence."

Government agencies keeping tabs on musicians is not new. The Nixon administration investigated former Beatle John Lennon in the 1970s and tried to have him deported. The band Body Count led by rapper Ice-T got the attention of police nationally in the early 1990s with the song Cop Killer. But those cases involved individual artists or groups, not monitoring across a musical genre.

"There's been no shortage of rock stars and other musicians" scrutinized by police, said Anthony DeCurtis, contributing editor at Rolling Stone magazine. "But there has never been anything like this."

Several music executives and legal scholars say the intelligence-gathering highlights the misunderstanding between the police and a $10-billion industry. The police, they contend, have used the slayings of high-profile artists like Tupac Shakur, the Notorious B.I.G and Run DMC's Jam Master Jay, to justify tracking many in the industry.

"Some people see gangs and hip-hop artists as being synonymous," said Benjamin Chavis, president and chief executive officer of The Hip-Hop Summit Action Network, a government-watchdog and voter-registration group. "That's a mistake. The recording industry is a legitimate American enterprise, not a gang."

Said attorney Bruce Rogow: "This kind of conduct shows insensitivity to constitutional limitations. It also implicates racial stereotyping."

Rogow successfully represented 2 Live Crew when the rap group was prosecuted for obscenity in the early '90s.

Part of Police Work

Press says it's good police work that has nothing to do with stereotyping a culture or musical genre: "What would law enforcement be if we closed our eyes. Our job is to know as much about things that could hurt innocent people."

Jeff Peel, director of Miami-Dade's Office of Film and Entertainment, said he's worried about a policy that could prompt hip-hop artists to stay away. South Florida is a choice spot for stars to live, celebrate and film music videos, an enterprise that pumps millions of dollars into the local economy.

"If something's going to dissuade them from coming, that would not be good news for us," Peel said.

Press and other officers say they welcome the musicians, but some rappers and their groups have had brushes with the law, police said. Miami Detective Peter Rosario said the practice of photographing rappers with their entourages shows who's in their circle.

"A lot if not most rappers belong to some sort of gang," Miami police Sgt. Rafael Tapanes said. "We keep track of their arrests and associates."

Dozens of rappers are tracked in the black binder, from minor artists like Black Rob to major figures like Sean "P. Diddy" Combs, Jay-Z, Nas and Busta Rhymes.

Publicists for Ja Rule, 50 Cent, Eminem, Jay-Z and P. Diddy refused to comment for this story.

Tapanes said the New York Police Department gave the binder to local law enforcement during a three-day "hip-hop training session" in May. Officers from other major cities like Los Angeles and Atlanta attended the event.

New York police officials denied having a hip-hop task force when asked recently by The Herald.

"What to Look for"

"Everybody that went got a binder with information on rappers that have been arrested, outlining charges," Tapanes said. "They were trained on what to look for in the lyrics, what to look for when they go to hip-hop concerts, what radio stations and TV stations to monitor to keep abreast of any rift between these rappers."

Press said local intelligence gathering on rap artists started after the Memorial Day 2001 weekend, when some 250,000 hip-hop fans flocked to South Beach for four days of parties hosted by their favorite rappers.

Beach police made 211 arrests, double the usual number of a regular weekend, most for disorderly conduct and intoxication.

No major rap artist was arrested, but police felt compelled to figure out every nuance of the hip-hop culture that had spawned such a following, said Press.

"Nobody on the Beach had a handle on who the players were," Press said. "We didn't know anything, we didn't know who were the big record labels, who were the kingpins; we didn't know why there were rivalries with Ja Rule and Eminem."

"It was paramount for us to understand because we know this is now their destination of choice," said Press, emphasizing that the department monitors activities related to other music events, including Spring Break festivities and this week's Winter Music Conference.

Besides the information they get from other police contacts, officers say they depend on hotel and nightclub workers and off-duty police officers on security details to keep them informed on the celebrities and their followers.

"If we know 50 Cent is coming to town then of course we have to be on alert," Press said. "We know there have been multiple attempts on his life."

The very notion that the Beach needed to send police to figure out the hip-hop culture is laughable, says Papa Keith, a DJ on 103.5 Tha Beat. "If they're saying they're trying to learn about hip-hop, then hire more brothers and put them in the ranks and let them help you in that respect," Keith said. "Why do you need to send a bunch of cops to New York?"

Of the Beach's 97 officers in supervisory jobs, only one is black. Of Miami's 226 ranking officers, 26 are black. Chavis, head of the HSAN, suggests sensitivity training for police departments.

Press says the fact that South Florida remains a destination for hip-hop artists and its fans proves that the police have not been heavy-handed.

Luther Campbell, the former 2 Live Crew rapper, said any intelligence gathering is unnecessary because rappers only come to South Florida to enjoy the weather and party.

"If they had problems like rappers coming down here and fighting, yeah you got to serve and protect," Campbell said. "But you don't have those kinds of problems. The cities should take taxpayer dollars and put them toward something else."

BEN YAGODA

Heavy Meta

The high point of my freshman-year English literature survey course, taught by that sweet man and Emily Dickinson biographer Richard Sewall, came early in the fall. Struggling through the Middle English of *The Canterbury Tales*, I arrived at the point in the story where the narrator of the poem—referred to by critics as "Chaucer the pilgrim"—becomes a character in it. At the conclusion of "The Prioress's Tale," the host notices "me" for the first time and asks, "What man artou? . . . Thou lookest as thou woldest find an hare, / For ever upon the ground I see thee stare." He asks Chaucer to contribute "a tale of mirth." The narrator replies that he knows only "a rym I lerned longe agoon." This turns out to be "The Tale of Sir Thopas," a turgid bit of doggerel about an ineffectual and effeminate knight. It goes on for a couple of dozen stanzas, and then, in the middle of a line, the host breaks in, hollering: "'Namore of this, for Goddes dignitee! . . . By God,' quod he, 'for plainly, at oo [one] word, / Thy drasty [rubbishy] rhyming is not worth a tord.'"

I found this thrilling, for reasons that weren't immediately clear. Turning to E. T. Donaldson's commentary in the back of my Chaucer book, I read, "The relation between the creator and the created that the situation implies is revealed by a mind almost godlike in the breadth and vision of its ironic vision." That was helpful. It led me to understand, in due time, that I responded powerfully in estimable works of art to moments when the artist . . . *winks*: acknowledges, implicitly or explicitly, that what we are experiencing is after all a piece of human handiwork and he or she is the creator of it. It is a gesture simultaneously of humility and of majesty, in both cases honoring the potency of art.

The next year, in a seminar on Romantic poetry, my ears pricked up highest in the discussion of the part in Keats's "Ode to a Nightingale" when he muses that the nightingale's song has "Charm'd magic casements, opening on the foam / Of perilous seas, in faery lands forlorn." The stanza ends, and the new one starts with, "Forlorn! the very word is like a bell / To toll me back from thee to my sole self!" The echoing of the word *forlorn*, the professor claimed (arguably but provocatively), was the first moment in the history of English verse that a poem took itself as its subject. In the final lecture of a Shakespeare survey, I got goose bumps when Alvin Kernan, another terrific teacher, recited the speech in which Prospero tells the audience that "The cloud-clapped towers, the gorgeous palaces, / The solemn temples, the great globe itself, / Yea, all which it inherit, shall dissolve, / And like this insubstantial pageant faded / Leave not a rack behind." The "great globe," he explained, was a reference to the Globe Theatre, where the play was being performed. Moreover, Prospero's forsaking his magic was implicitly compared to Shakespeare himself giving up the magic of play-writing, *The Tempest* being his final work. And moreover (not to put too fine a point on it), this was Kernan's final lecture, before leaving teaching for administrative work, so we understood that he, too, was implicitly saying he was giving up his magic. Great stuff.

All this happened in the 1970s, when postmodernism was barely a concept. Now it's a frayed cultural cliché. The self-reference I responded to in Chaucer and Shakespeare long ago acquired an academic moniker—"reflexivity." A related phenomenon, works referring to *other* works, was dubbed "intertextuality." Together they are subsumed under the ubiquitous term "meta," at one time a useful prefix for self-conscious endeavors, now an annoying, nearly all-purpose adjective. ("*The Matrix* is very meta.") Practice has, if anything, outstripped theory. Plays that break the fourth wall, sitcoms about comedians playing themselves, movies (like *Adaptation*) about the process of making a movie, buildings or paintings or poems or novels that refer to themselves as buildings or paintings or poems or novels: we have all, probably, had enough of them.

But I still respond to—indeed, delight in—reflexivity and intertextuality in one art form. That would be popular music. Flipping the radio dial, I get chills when I come on James Taylor's "That's Why I'm Here" ("Fortune and fame's such a curious game / Perfect strangers can call you by name / Pay good money to hear 'Fire and Rain' / Again and again and again"), or the Beatles' "Glass Onion" ("I told you 'bout Strawberry Fields, / You know the place where nothing is real"), Pink's "Don't Let Me Get Me" ("Tired of being compared to / Damn Britney Spears / She's so pretty / That just ain't me"), or even Eminem's "White America" ("Let's do the math. / If I was black, I would've sold half"). And I actually grin when a country station plays a recent hit by Alan Jackson that's about, and is, a "Three Minute Positive Not Too Country Uptempo Love Song." For years—decades—I have been collecting these songs, just as bird-watchers do with their sightings, separating my life list into categories and subcategories, and ranking all entries according to originality, profundity, and ultimate value.

I will share my system with you in a minute, as soon as I try to rebut the charge that self-reference in pop music does *not* escape the curses of preciousness, self-regard, cliché, and portentousness it is subject to elsewhere. A clue to its avoidance strategy is the word itself: the music—the melody, the singing, the instrumentation, the beat—takes attention and a portion of the burden from the words. This phenomenon is one of the glorious things about popular music. The words to a song may lie leaden on the page in a CD booklet or an ill-conceived *Collected Lyrics*, but, through a strange alchemy, reverberate like poetry when they are accompanied by melody. In the same way, the music can remove the self-importance from a level of reflexivity that, drunk neat, would be deadly.

American popular song lyrics have always had a wide self-conscious streak. Possibly the most successful popular song of all time was Irving Berlin's 1911 "Alexander's Ragtime Band," a song about music. Ira Gershwin's first lyrics to be sung in public, in 1918, were to "The Real American Folk Song Is a Rag"; a later effort was "What Can You Say in a Love Song (That Hasn't Been Said Before)?" from the musical comedy "Life Begins at 8:40," beginning "Darling, here's that song you inspired / In a style I acquired / Living with songs of the past." Gershwin and the other inhabitants of Tin Pan Alley, the mythical locus of the popular songwriting industry, continually nudged one another in the ribs with reminders of what it was they were doing. The Alley was a closed cosmos, with songs commenting on predecessors and begetting successors: first, "Meet Me Tonight in Dreamland," then "When I Met You Tonight in Dreamland" and "Dreamland Brings Memories of You."

The great American songwriters, all of whom either started on Tin Pan Alley or were begotten by it, liked to tip their hats to one another. In "They Can't Take That Away from Me," Gershwin name-checks one of Irving Berlin's classics: "The song is ended, but as the songwriter wrote / 'The Melody Lingers On.'" Berlin, who normally looked straight ahead in his lyrics, permitted himself, "Tuneful, tasteful, soulful, smart. / Music: Rodgers. Lyrics: Hart." In "You're the Top," Cole Porter paired "Waldorf salad" with "Berlin ballad" and referred to "gifted humans like Vincent Youmans," surely one of the all-time great rhymes. It was Porter who took this sort of thing beyond intramural bantering to high wit. He wrote the immortal couplet "But how strange / The change from major to minor," which is sung just as the key of the song ("Every Time We Say Goodbye") *changes from major to minor*. "It's De-Lovely," from the musical "Anything Goes," begins, "I feel a sudden urge to sing / The kind of ditty that invokes the spring. / So control your desire to curse / While I crucify the verse. / This verse I've started seems to me / The 'Tin-Pan-tithesis' of melody. / So to spare you all the pain, / I'll skip the darn thing and sing the refrain." Tin-Pan-tithesis: the formulation deserves a moment of silence.

Hoagy Carmichael's "Stardust," which some authorities consider the greatest American song, is *about* a melody that, the singer tells us, "haunts my reverie . . . Now my consolation / Is in the stardust of a song." Is the song "Stardust"? It's a mystery, but a sweet one.

Tin Pan Alley was zoned out of existence a long time ago. But today's generically striated pop universe—country, hip-hop, rock, and so forth, each with its own further gradations—is just as self-referential. In fact, it's more so, and in order to assess the field adequately I'll need to break it into two groups, the reflexive and the intertextual, each with a meta offshoot.

The first category consists of songs that refer to or are about themselves, in the manner of "Ode to a Nightingale" and "It's De-Lovely." And so: Elton John's "Your Song"; James Taylor's "Hey Mister, That's Me Up On the Jukebox" ("I'm the one who's singing this sad song"); Brooks and Dunn's "I Used to Know This Song By Heart"; George Harrison's "This Song" (the two-word phrase occurs in most of these entries); Simon and Garfunkel's "Song for the Asking"; Carly Simon's "You're So Vain" ("You probably think this song is about you"); The Doors' "Hello, I Love You" ("When she moves, my brain sings out this song"); Jim Croce's "I'll Have to Say I Love You in a Song"; Public Enemy's "Bring the Noise" ("Radio stations I question their blackness / They call themselves black, / But we'll see if they play *this*"); Three Dog Night's "Old-Fashioned Love Song"; Spandau Ballet's "True" ("Why do I find it hard to write the next line?"); Steely Dan's "Deacon Blues" ("I cried when I wrote this song / Sue me if I play too long"); the American Music Club's "I Broke My Promise" ("That I wouldn't write another song about you. / I guess I lied"); the Beatles' "Only a Northern Song" ("If you're listening to this song / You may think the chords are going wrong") and "Michelle" ("These are words that go together well").

One thing should be immediately apparent from the list: reflexiveness can be associated with both good and bad songs. You don't have to be familiar with every title to grasp that, merely with the two biggest chart-busters, by Elton John and Three Dog Night. "Old-Fashioned Love Song" is a bland and genial ditty, saved—barely—from complete negligibility by its self-reference. Bernie Taupin's lyrics to "Your Song," swept along by John's potent melody, are, like many lyric poems, convincingly about the challenges of doing justice in words to the loved one's qualities. Toward the end, they double in on themselves in true "Forlorn! The very word is like a bell" fashion, the singer admitting, haltingly, "You see I've forgotten if they're green or they're blue. / Anyway the thing is, what I really mean, / Yours are the sweetest eyes I've ever seen."

There's nothing special or mysterious about what makes good self-conscious songs good—just adequate artistry, originality, wit, and feeling. The last is especially important, but the other qualities can go a long way as well. The rapper Nas does some dazzlingly reflexive sleight of hand, in the braggadocious mode hip-hop has claimed for its own, when he raps, "They shootin! / Aw, made you look. / You a slave to a page in my rhyme book."

In this subgenre, the song about itself, one trope has inspired some particularly ingenious lyric writing: imagining the effect the song will have on listeners when it comes out of the radio or, especially in country music, the jukebox. (The inanimate object vibrating with the song is reminiscent of the Aeolian Harp or Lyre, a common image in Romantic poetry: the winds of the world would blow through it and make haunting melodies.) The country singer David Allan Coe has a number called "I'm Going to Hurt Her on the Radio," and Buck Owens's 1979 song "Play 'Together Again' Again" asks a bystander to put in a quarter and punch the numbers of an earlier Owens hit. Bruce Springsteen's moving "Bobby Jean," addressed to a friend or lover who's unexpectedly taken a powder, conjectures: "Maybe you'll be out there on that road / Somewhere in some bus or train / Traveling along in some motel room / There'll be a radio playing and you'll hear me sing this song. / Well, if you do, you'll know I'm thinking of you."

Loudon Wainwright III's mordant "Pretty Good Day" is a catalogue of small victories. The singer wakes up and finds that the water is running. He walks through the streets without hearing any sirens or getting shot or even seeing any snipers, and when he gets home, he says, "Nobody was frightened, wounded, hungry, or cold." The final stanza is unanticipatedly cathartic: "I slept through the night, got through to the dawn / I flipped the switch and the light went on. / I wrote down my dream, I wrote this song." Those last four words turn the closing refrain—"It's a pretty good day so far"—from ironic self-protection to a welcome truth.

None of the lyrical maneuvers or tropes I've described above should be unfamiliar to past or present English majors, who would do well to equip their computers with a global key that produces the phrase, "Just as in the poem . . . " Indeed, it is accepted wisdom that reflexivity is an, if not *the*, obsession of modern poetry. You find it explicitly in, for example, Archibald MacLeish's "Arts Poetica" ("A poem should not mean / But be"), and implicitly pretty much wherever you look—in Pound, Eliot, Stevens. But there's an advanced class of pop-music reflexivity that is little seen in these poets, although, come to think of it, it's everywhere in Whitman, who even gave it a name: "Song of Myself." In popular music, this is a post-Beatles phenomenon. In the pre-rock era, a popular singer—think Frank Sinatra—was manifestly an actor, convincingly giving voice to the playwright's (songwriter's) words and music. One of the few figures who combined singing and songwriting (as well as a capacious ego) was George M. Cohan, and his work was full of explicitly autobiographical representations, most famously in "The Yankee Doodle Boy."

Now singers and bands are expected to have composed their own material, and the Cohan stance is standard. Most blatantly, there is the song about the singer or singers: sometimes merely saying his, her, or their name, sometimes promoting, sometimes defending, sometimes narrating. For some reason, the one that always comes to mind is the Monkees' theme song, the one that starts, "Hey, hey, we're the Monkees." (Surely Grandmaster Flash and the Furious Five were paying homage to those boys in "The Message" when they rapped, "Hey, we're Grandmaster Flash and the Furious Five." A later rap ensemble kicked it up a notch and weren't paying homage to anybody in a song piquantly titled, "Wu-Tang Clan Ain't Nuthing to **** Wit"). But there are many others. The late-seventies band Devo memorably chanted, "Are we not men? / We are Devo!" The Mamas and the Papas' "Creeque Alley" is a musical memoir in the form of a shaggy-dog story: "John and Mitchy were getting kind of itchy / Just to leave the folk music behind / Zol and Denny workin' for a penny / Tryin' to get a fish on the line." John Lennon and his wife, Yoko Ono, sang "The Ballad of John and Yoko," just as Mott the Hoople sang "The Ballad of Mott the Hoople." Grand Funk Railroad protested too much in "We're an American Band," and Jennifer Lopez recently used autobiography as spin control when she tried to convince her longtime fans that despite all the magazine covers and bling-bling, she was still "Jenny from the Block." John Eddie has a painfully funny recent song about a special circle of hell for the singer-songwriter: the bar where a drunk loudly asks, "Who the Hell is John Eddie?" (The title of the song is the heckler's command—"Play Some Skynyrd.") The blustery "I Write the Songs" indulged in enough egotism to taint both the author (Bruce Johnston of the Beach Boys) and the bellower of the highest-charting version (Barry Manilow). Moving from the ridiculous to the sublime: It isn't surprising that thoughtful singer-songwriters like Neil Young, Joni Mitchell, Merle Haggard, and Paul Simon would have produced rich meditations about music's significance to them, in, respectively, "From Hank to Hendrix," "For Free," "After I Sing My Songs," and "Old."

A subtle, off-center kind of introspection can be found in the alter-ego song or group of songs, presented in the voice of a performer who has something but not everything in common with the actual one: the Beatles' "Sgt. Pepper's Lonely Hearts Club Band," Dire Straits' "Sultans of Swing," Eminem's Slim Shady,

David Bowie's Ziggy Stardust, Billy Joel's "Piano Man." Glen Campbell has bookended his career with two such songs (neither of which he wrote): the 1975 "Rhinestone Cowboy," in which an unknown dreams of "getting cards and letters from people I don't even know," and the more recent "Mansion in Bronson," in which the record company tells an aging country star, "You're too out of shape for Wranglers and too old for videos." A small masterpiece in the subgenre is Randy Newman's "Lonely at the Top," whose singer, evidently a show-biz icon, boasts, "I've been around the world / Had my pick of any girl." Newman wrote this when he was a struggling songwriter and performer with no albums to his credit.

I actually prefer autobiographical moments to autobiographical songs. In "You Gotta Serve Somebody," Dylan (né Robert Zimmerman), normally unforthcoming to the point of invisibility, shockingly proclaims, "You may call me Bobby, you may call me Zimmy." In "Tenth Avenue Freezeout," Springsteen recalls "When they made that change uptown and the Big Man joined the band." The Big Man: saxophonist and crowd favorite Clarence Clemons; in concert, the line always gets a roar. James Taylor's "Fire and Rain" talks about "Sweet dreams and flying machines." Flying Machine: Taylor's first band. A great moment in the Supremes' "Back in My Arms Again" comes when lead singer Diana Ross interrupts her romantic lament to wonder, "How can Mary tell me what to do / When she lost her love so true? / And Flo, she don't know / 'Cause the boy she loves is a Romeo." Mary and Flo: fellow Supremes Mary Wilson and Florence Birdsong. One puzzling but cool thing about the aside is that it (like the rest of the song) wasn't written by Ross but by Motown staff composers Holland-Dozier-Holland. In "Showbiz Kids," Steely Dan throws in an unexpected self-reference in the manner of a Hitchcock cameo or a postage-stamp portrait-of-the-artist in a vast landscape: "They got the Steely Dan T-shirts."

When it comes to singing about yourself, the hands-down champions are two musical forms that are rarely, if ever, associated with each other: country and hip-hop. They show up disproportionately in all these categories, in fact; one reason is that they still prize the Tin Pan Alley values of wordplay and wit. In keeping with the rhyming toasts and dozens of the African-American oral tradition, rap is partial to boasts about the rapper's prowess in rhyming, loving, fighting, etc. Thus Run-DMC raps, "I'm the king of rock, there ain't none higher / Sucker MCs should call me sire." In another number, Run-DMC gives its deejay, Jam Master Jay (since deceased), his props: "J-A-Y are the letters of his name / Cuttin' and scratchin' are the aspects of his game, / So check out the Master as he cuts these jams / And look at us with the mikes in our hands."

Early country performers tended to sing their hymns of love, memory, and heartbreak through generic personae, although Jimmie Rodgers had a song about himself called "Jimmie the Kid" and Ernest Tubb one called "When I First Began to Sing," which cited Rodgers as an influence. The greatest country singer was Hank Williams. The power of his lyrics lay in their seemingly complete emotional sincerity; it was chilling that at the time of his death in 1953, he was on the charts with a song called "I'll Never Get Out of This World Alive." But he made few, if any, direct references to himself—ironic, considering how obsessively he has been invoked by others. Modern country autobiography began in 1971, when Johnny Cash recorded "The Man in Black," which explained his wardrobe ("I wear it for the thousands who have died, / Believin' that the Lord was on their side," among other reasons), and Loretta Lynn recorded "Coal Miner's Daughter," which told the story of Loretta Lynn's life. Both songs gave their creators indelible nicknames—and nicknames are very, very big in country.

The floodgates opened with the "outlaw country" movement a couple of years later, which took as its text Kitty Wells's old number "The Life They Live in Songs." Willie "Red-Headed Stranger" Nelson and Waylon "Hoss" Jennings, in particular, laid bare the big and small concerns of their existence. Nelson spun picaresque yarns like "On the Road Again," "Me and Paul," and "Devil in a Sleeping Bag" and angrily told greedy record-company executives to "Write Your Own Songs"; Jennings asked rhetorically, "Don't You Think This Outlaw Bit's Done Got Out of Hand?" and "Are You Sure Hank Done It This Way?"

The laureate of country memoir is Hank Williams Jr., also known as Bocephus, who was just three years old when his father died. As a child, he went on the road singing Hank Williams songs, in an uncanny imitation of Hank Williams's voice. The experience was unenviable, but it provided young Bocephus with a great theme. In 1966, when Hank Jr. was seventeen, he wrote and recorded "Standing in the Shadows": "I know I'm not great, and some say I imitate. . . . It's hard when you're standing in the shadows of a very famous man." He struggled with this burden over the next decade, and in the late 1970s and early '80s issued a series of compelling songs—including "The Conversation," "Living Proof," and "Whisky Bent and Hellbound"—about trying to live up to his father's musical standards and at the time escape the legacy of a self-destructive life and early death. His masterpiece, I would say, is "Family Tradition," where the refrain alternates between a lament and a sort of rueful and rollicking celebration: "Lord, I have loved some ladies and I have loved Jim Beam / And they both tried to kill me in 1973. / When that doctor asked me, / 'Son how did you get in this condition?' / I said, 'Hey sawbones, I'm just carrying on / An ole family tradition.'"

The autobiographical expectation in country has become sufficiently entrenched as to spawn ghostwriters. That is, everyone in Nashville knows that George "Possum" Jones doesn't write his own songs, but, as a significant singer with a troubled past, he is expected to sing about himself. Therefore, other writers regularly supply him with numbers that allow him to poke fun at his own image, like "I Don't Need Your Rocking Chair" and "(They Call Me) No-Show Jones." I have no problem with that, but the self-mythologizing of minor figures, like David Allen Coe in "Waylon, Willie, and Me," can get wearing.

"Waylon, Willie, and Me": The song is also an example of the second broad category, musical intertextuality, where the references are to *other* compositions and performers. Unavoidable examples are Don McLean's "American Pie" and Rick Nelson's "Garden Party," rather self-satisfied allegories that all but demand crib sheets to parse the references, (In "American Pie," "the King" is Elvis and "the Jester" is Dylan—but who's "the Queen"?) By contrast, a single well-placed musical allusion can be the brushstroke that lifts a song out of the ordinary: see Mary Chapin Carpenter's "there ain't no cure for my blues today / Except when the paper says Beausoleil is coming to town"; Springsteen's "Roy Orbison sang for the lonely"; Stephen Bishop's "put on Sinatra and start to cry"; Nirvana's "Give me a Leonard Cohen afterworld / So I can sigh eternally"; Steely Dan's "Hey Nineteen" ("that's 'Retha Franklin / She don't remember the Queen of Soul"); Calexico's song "Not Even Stevie Nicks"; the Police's line "An Otis Redding record, it's all I own," and Davis Daniel's "She went to William and Mary, / I went to Haggard and Jones."

Earlier, I mentioned some early Tin Pan Alley "response" songs, and that continuing tradition definitely supplies an intertextual frisson. In 1954, an R & B singer named Hank Ballard put out a suggestive record, full of double entendres, called "Work with Me, Annie." It was so successful that it crossed over to the pop charts, and Ballard and his band, the Midnighters, followed it up with "Annie Had a Baby (Can't Work No More)," "Annie's Aunt Fannie," and "Henry's Got Flat Feet (Can't Dance No More)." Others got into the act as well, most notably Etta James, in "Roll with Me, Henry." (A white singer, Georgia Gibbs, released a sanitized version, "Dance with Me, Henry.") That kind of call-and-response is a sign of vitality and attentiveness in the art form.

It can be even more invigorating when song number two begs to differ with song number one. Hank Thompson's reflexive 1951 "The Wild Side of Life" starts with the lament that since the singer's wife has abandoned him, he must give her his message "in the words of this song." And the message is, "The glamour of the gay night life has lured you / To the places where the wine and liquor flows." Kitty Wells's response came swiftly, and constituted a rousing pre-feminism feminist statement: "As I sit here tonight, the juke box playing / That old song about the wild, wild side of life. / As I listen to the words you are saying, / It brings memories when I was a trusting wife. / It wasn't God who made honky-tonk angels / As you say in the words of your song." UTFO's early rap song "Roxanne, Roxanne" inspired some twenty-five responses, including two by singers who adopted the name of the girl in the song and told her side of the story: Roxanne Shante and the Real Roxanne. Merle Haggard's "Okie from Muskogee" spawned Big Brother and the Holding Company's "I'll Fix Your Flat Tire, Merle" and "Up Against the Wall, Redneck Mother," written by Ray Wylie Hubbard and performed by Jerry Jeff Walker. And who can forget Lynyrd Skynyrd's "Sweet Home, Alabama": "I hope Neil Young will remember / Southern man don't need him around anyhow"?

As this suggests, response songs can move beyond disagreement to assault and battery. In a sour mood, John Lennon asked Paul McCartney, "How Do You Sleep?" ("The freaks was right when they said you was dead,") Richard Thompson's "I Agree with Pat Metheny" refers to Metheny's outburst against saxophonist Kenny G's digitized "duet" with Louis Armstrong: "A meeting of the minds, how nice / Like Einstein and Sporty Spice." Joan Baez got Dylan—"the unwashed phenomenon, the original vagabond"—most famously in "Diamonds and Rust," but stuck the knife in a little deeper in "Oh Brother," which begins "You've got eyes like Jesus / But you speak with a viper's tongue." They Might Be Giants' catty "Rhythm Section Want Ad" asks "Do you sing like Olive Oyl on purpose? / You guys must be into the Eurythmics." John Hiatt's "Memphis in the Morning," a rare anti-country-music song, correctly observes, "I don't think Ronnie Milsap's ever going to record this song."

The genre that thrives on insults—also known as "beefs"—is, of course, rap, where it's understood that the more derisively a performer can put down a competitor, the more decisively he can elevate himself. The still-unsolved murders of the feuding Tupac Shakur and the Notorious B.I.G. several years ago put a bit of a damper on all-out beefing, but it has returned in a stylized and presumably stage-managed form, reminiscent of show-business rows like the one between Jack Benny and Fred Allen. So, Nelly on KRS-One: "You the first old man should get a rapper's pension / No hits since the cordless mic invention." Nas's "Ether" asked Jay-Z, "How much of Biggie's rhymes is gonna come out your fat lips?"; Jay-Z responded with "Super Ugly," which bragged of his affair with the mother of Nas's daughter. Eazy-E took on a major hip-hop figure with "All of a sudden Dr. Dre is a g-thing / But on his old album covers, he was a she-thing." ("G" is short for *gangsta*.) Not exactly Oscar Wilde, but it works for me.

Country music, by contrast, favors an intertextuality of admiration, most visibly in the tribute song. To be sure, country has no monopoly on this sometimes moving, sometimes schmaltzy, sometimes crass genre. Ronnie McDowell recorded "The King Is Gone" the day after Elvis Presley's death, and it's been followed by 202 more Elvis tributes, according to New York deejay Peter Bochan, who lists them on his Web site (http://www.mixedup.com/elvissongs.htm). If there's a "Rock and Roll Heaven," the Righteous Brothers memorably noted, "you know they've got a hell of a band." George Harrison sang about John Lennon in "All Those Years Ago," and Ringo Starr in turn memorialized George in "Never Without You." The Commodores' "Night Shift" honors the estimable lineup of fallen soul singers, and Tupac Shakur has been mourned in Master P's "Is There a Heaven 4 a Gangsta?," Richie Rich's "Do G's Go to Heaven?," and Naughty By Nature's "Mourn Till I Join Ya," which avers, "Nigga I miss ya this thug gonna miss ya till I'm witcha."

But this is as nothing compared with country tribute songs. The tradition started in 1933, with the death of the Singing Brakeman, Jimmie Rodgers, at the age of thirty-five. Just days later, "When Jimmie Rodgers Said Goodbye" was issued, followed by "The Train Carrying Jimmie Rodgers Home," "The Life of Jimmie Rodgers," "The Passing of Jimmie Rodgers," and many others. Hank Williams's death twenty years later, at the age of twenty-nine, was followed by a veritable flood of tributes. According to the critic Christopher Metress, sixteen songs honoring Williams were released in 1953 alone, and there has been no sign of a letup. A German devotee of American country music lists ninety-six Williams tribute songs on his Web site (http://www.haukestruebing.com), including "Hank Williams Meets Jimmie Rodgers," "Hank Williams Sings the Blues No More," "Please Don't Let the Name 'Hank' Die," "Everybody Wants to Be Hank Williams," Jerry Jeff Walker's "I Feel Like Hank Williams Tonight," and Johnny Cash's "The Night Hank Williams Came to Town."

Country songwriters love tribute songs so much that they even write them to singers who are still alive, as in David Allan Coe's "Hank Williams Jr."; Toby Keith's "I'll Never Smoke Weed with Willie Again"; Tim McGraw's "Give It to Me Strait"; Chris Wall's "An Outlaw's Blues," about Waylon Jennings; Becky Hollis's "Jones on the Jukebox"; and Daryle Singletary's "That's Why I Sing This Way" (the reason, he explains, is "Mama used to whip me with a George Jones album"). Before his death in September 2003, Johnny Cash was the subject of "(In the Mood for) Johnny Cash," "Hooked on Johnny Cash," "Walking Talking Johnny Cash Blues," Billy Joe Shaver's "That's Why the Man in Black Sings the Blues," and his own daughter Roseanne's lovely "My Old Man."

If you sing a song of a certain kind, if your parents sang that song, and if you expect that your children will sing it as well, then you're not likely to attempt to characterize, explain, or defend it *in* a song. But sometimes a musical genre is more contentious. Listeners and performers think about and define themselves by it. That the blues is a highly self-conscious genre can be grasped merely from the fact that roughly half of blues songs contain the word *blues* in their title. The merits of rock and roll were lyrically proclaimed seemingly from the moment of its birth, the constant invocation of "rock" and "rock and roll" being only partly explained by the terms' sexual innuendo. Bill

Haley and the Comets asked us to "Rock Around the Clock"; Chuck Berry wrote a song (covered by the Beatles) called, simply, "Rock and Roll Music" and in another commanded, "Hail, hail rock and roll"; Danny and the Juniors proclaimed "Rock and Roll Is Here to Stay." Meanwhile, rearguard singers vocally demurred, as Nat King Cole in "Mr. Cole Won't Rock and Roll," which regretfully observed, "When Tin Pan Alley serenades a beauty / Do they sing of Rose Marie or Sweet Lorraine? / No, they dedicate a hymn to Tutti Frutti, / Who's as tender as a dame from Mickey Spillane." The Byrds' "So You Want To Be a Rock and Roll Star" was a biographical mock-epic. The modest rhetoric of the Rolling Stones' 1974 "It's Only Rock and Roll (But I Like It)" was appropriate, since the battle had long been won, although heavy-metal anthems of the late '70s and early '80s, such as AC/DC's "Let There Be Rock," protested excessively in invoking rock (never rock and roll) as a near-holy pursuit. And, needless to say, there will never be an end to boring songs about life on the road.

When it comes to meta-music, yet again, country is king. There is a curious history here. As Richard A. Peterson explains in his 1997 book *Creating Country Music*, the word *country* itself was an invention of the early 1950s. The music had been called, variously, "western," "hillbilly," and "folk"; to consolidate the terms and, Peterson shows, to avoid the left-wing associations with the last (Pete Seeger and Paul Robeson performed folk music, after all), the Nashville powers that be concocted "country." It was an immediate and permanent success, largely, I would say, because it brilliantly combined a declaration of the rural origin of the music with a subliminal patriotic assertion: that the music was of, about, and for *this* country.

Whatever the reasons, the country song about country music has become legion. A partial, alphabetical list, including only ones that put the magic word in the title:

"Back When Country Was Ugly"; "Country Enough"; "Country in My Genes"; "Country Music Is Here to Stay"; "Country My Ass"; "Country Till I Die"; "Country Was the

Song"; "A Damn Good Country Song"; "Don't Think You're Too Good for Country Music"; "Every Kind of Music But Country"; "A Few Old Country Boys"; "Gone Country"; "Heart of a Country Song"; "Here's to Country Music"; "Hit Country Song"; "I Was Country When Country Wasn't Cool"; "If That Ain't Country"; "If There Was No Country Music"; "I'm Country"; "I'm That Country"; "A Jukebox with a Country Song"; "Kindly Keep It Country"; "My Life Would Make a Damn Good Country Song"; "Now That's Country"; "The Perfect Country Song"; "Put Some Drive in Your Country"; "A Sad Country Song"; "Take Me Back to the Country"; "Too Country"; "Too Rock for Country"; "Welcome to the Country Music Hall of Fame"; and "You're Looking at Country."

There are three broad historical categories. The first were self-congratulatory: songs about how wonderful Jimmie, Hank, and Lefty were; how the singer is following in their path; how there's nothing like a country song to express joy or heartbreak. The second, more contentious and dating from the 1970s, recognized that a debate had opened up about the very meaning of "country music." Southern rock bands like Lynyrd Skynyrd and the Allman Brothers had claimed a kinship with country, to the dismay of some venerable Nashville personages, and the outlaws—Hoss, Willie, Bocephus, the Man in Black, and Kris Kristofferson—countered with pleas for a more inclusive definition. One of Hank Jr.'s several entries in this category, "Why Don't You Leave Them Boys Alone?" (cowritten with Tanya Tucker), was noteworthy because he was joined on it not only by Waylon Jennings but also by one of the old guard, Ernest Tubb.

The third, still-current type is a lament, summed up in the lyrics of the Dixie Chicks' recent hit "Long Time Gone": "the music ain't got no soul / Now they sound tired but they don't sound Haggard / They've got money but they don't have Cash. / They got Junior but they don't have Hank." Or, in the title of a Travis Tritt song, "Country Ain't Country." The villains of these pieces aren't rock bands but the likes of Billy Ray Cyrus, Garth Brooks, Faith Hill, and Shania Twain: the cowboy-hatted, midriff-baring Barbie and Ken dolls whose bland and innocuous sounds push *real* country artists off the so-called country stations. Performers like Tritt, Alan Jackson, Vince Gill, and Marty Stuart include at least one such critique on every CD they release. Stuart is the most self-consciously militant of this group. His most recent recording is called *Country Music*, which is a little like Jonathan Franzen putting out a novel called *Contemporary Fiction*.

Have I justified my obsession? If not, it's probably too late to defend it. But I will say that as fatuous, lame, inauthentic, and cheesy as popular music often is, it manages to retain a gravity not often found in other arts, low or high. The way people respond to an action movie, a prime-time soap opera, or a romance novel can be fairly easily dismissed, as the fulfillment of cut-rate fantasy or some other article of bad faith. Music's logic is at its base emotional and thus not as easily assailed. More elevated works—say, an off-off-Broadway play in which the actors start commenting on the previous scene, or a contemporary painting that, in its use of color or texture, is "about" painting—have a contrary problem: they are trees falling in, if not a forest, then a very sparsely populated region. In pop music, good or bad, there is usually the sense that something is at stake. As a result, it demands our attention. Bob Dylan is no Shakespeare, but, like Shakespeare, he appears to be putting a great deal on the line. In the song "Sara," Dylan sings of "staying up for days in the Chelsea Hotel, / Writing 'Sad-Eyed Lady of the Lowlands' for you." That puts me, for one, in mind of Prospero. At one point near the end of Neil Young's recent rock comic-opera, "Greendale," where all the parts are sung by Young, the character "Grampa" erupts with a complaint: "That guy just keeps singin'! / Can somebody shut him up? / I don't know for the life of me / where he comes up with that stuff." For my money, that's a moment of comic and cosmic humility that ranks up there with "The Tale of Sir Thopas."

TOM ROCHE

There Is a Light That Never Goes Out

And so we begin at the end.

John Peel, the legendary broadcaster, master communicator, perpetual adolescent, and champion of three generations of unsigned bands, died at 65 on October 25, 2004.

He did what would turn out to be his last Radio 1 show on October 14, featuring the usual fascinating genre collision of the up-to-date and vintage, the obscure and the memorable, the same way he had presented this unique parade continually since 1967.

Peel's playlist that Thursday would, as usual, send a Clear Channel programmer into an apoplectic fit: Techno-chill from DJ Preach, full-throttle rock from the Detroit Cobras, and yet another fresh new Peel Session. The exclusive session guests this time, joining hundreds of others over the decades, was the unsigned grindcore band Trencher (with their new songs "I Lost All My Hair in a Skiing Accident" and "Trapped Under a Train Alive.") Trencher, a band so new and obscure that a websearch returns nothing, was soon followed by an actual Conway Twitty 78, and John also dug out regular favorites Jimmy Reed, and the Fall's "Powder Keg."

His last song was by the amazing electro-innovators Klute, called "Time 4 Change" from their new LP *No One's Listening Anymore* on, tellingly, the Commercial Suicide label.

Although he sounded as lively and as happy as ever on air, by some accounts he was overworked and made weary by a schedule that would burden a person half his age. While programming and presenting three two-hour BBC shows weekly, a weekly spoken-word hour on Radio 4, a weekly music show on World Service and shows for small European networks, he somehow kept track of the hundreds of new demos arriving every month from unsigned bands. Not to mention his role as a busy and devoted father of four. And, lastly, he was in receipt of a £1 million advance to write his definitive autobiography, a task he could barely find time to begin. So John, along with Sheila, his wife of 30 years, set out on a three-week vacation to Peru as a much-needed break.

A few days later, John phoned the BBC from Peru to tell his young producers all was fine, and could someone go on the internet and look up where the best record stores are in Lima? Later that week he journeyed to the town of Cuzco, Peru, high in the Andean Mountains. After an uneventful day, John was preparing for dinner when he suffered a massive heart attack.

The attending physician, Dr. Alcides Vargas, told Peruvian Radio, "Mr. Peel was lying on the floor in the (hotel) lobby, and his wife Sheila was crying uncontrollably. There was complete hysteria. We had medical equipment like defibrillators and a ventilator. But there were no vital signs."

Dr. Vargas said the thin air of the city of Cuzco, some 11,000 feet above sea level, almost certainly triggered John's fatal attack. (Peel had been diagnosed as diabetic in 2001, a condition that can quietly elevate heart risks.)

Back in Britain, the outpouring was immediate and overwhelming: Over 5,000 messages of condolences to the BBC web site within three hours, and 30,000 tributes from all over the world were sent by the end of the week. Radio 1 scrapped all regular programming for the day. The tribute issue of *NME* said it best: "John Peel 1939–2004—Hero, Legend, Good Bloke."

It was a sudden, tragic end to a fascinating life story, full of both ambition and the lack of it, strange detours, and simple twists of fate.

Liverpool

John Robert Parker Ravenscroft (his real name) was born near Liverpool, England, Aug. 30, 1939, the son of a well-off textile broker. In his early school years, Peel was, admittedly, quite unmotivated, as evidenced by a note attached to his report card one day. John once recalled, "At my primary school (and bear in mind that my name is John) the headmistress wrote, 'Robin has failed to make much impression this term.'"

Later, "People said to me (at high school), 'If you don't work hard you won't go to university.' I assumed university would just be an extension of public school, and, at the time, it would have been. So I thought: thank you for telling me that. So I didn't work and didn't go." "You had so little control over your life" in that regimented British upbringing, he said. "Maybe failure was the only instrument of control you had."

It wasn't even the 1960s and yet Peel was already dropping out. He sought out non-BBC radio fare such as American Forces Radio from Europe. "The first time I heard Little Richard, I was actually frightened by it—you could not believe such an intense and simple noise could be coming out of your radio. It was like Saul on the road to Damascus, a life-changing experience." One schoolmate at the time was Michael Palin, who would eventually be a co-founder of Monty Python's Flying Circus. Says Palin, "I remember him lying on his back in his study, listening to, I guess it was, skiffle. Even then he introduced us to music he'd never heard. Even then he was a rebel, an independent voice."

From 1957 to 1959 he was drafted into the Army as a radar operator in the Royal Artillery. He noted later, "The Army said afterwards, 'At no time has he shown any sign of adapting to the military way of life.' I took it as a compliment."

Texas

Peel's father had business contacts in Texas, and offered to send Peel there in 1960, where the contacts treated him as cheap labor. He then took a brief stint selling door-to-door insurance, and around this time, incredibly, he was in Dallas on November 22, 1963, the day John F. Kennedy was assassinated. Out of curiosity, he went to the Dallas police station and bluffed his way into Lee Harvey Oswald's arraignment hearing, claiming in a heavy accent that he was a reporter for *The Liverpool Echo*. "I then went and made what I'd said retrospectively true and phoned *The Liverpool Echo* to give them the story. But they didn't care. I was a bit wounded by that."

Old newsreel films of the event show Jack Ruby to have been in the room also, and Peel standing off in a corner. Peel remembers, "In a documentary they showed on British television, the camera pans across the room to show Ruby, and in the last few frames, me and my friend Bob are standing there, looking like tourists."

Peel's only respite from the insurance racket was the Dallas Top 40 stations. When the Beatles hit, one DJ—WRR's Russ "Weird Beard" Knight—began cluelessly talking up England and Liverpool, ". . . and complete nonsense. I phoned him up, and he put me on the air as 'Our Man from Liverpool.'" After a few weeks of on-air call-ins Peel was offered a weekend job.

His first full-time radio gig was at KOMA in Oklahoma City in 1965. "Americans thought Europe was the size of a village, so they assumed anyone from Liverpool was a close personal friend of Ringo."

California

Peel moved to San Bernardino, an hour outside of L.A. in 1966, landing a gig at tiny KMEN-AM. The winds of change sweeping the Southern California music scene were having an effect on regimented Top 40 radio formats. The Doors, Frank Zappa, Love, and Quicksilver were abandoning the three-minute hit single format for extended innovations, but would radio "play" along?

Around this time, a younger-than-she-looked music fan became a groupie of some of KMEN's eclectic DJs, offering various services, services Peel has declined to name. Unbeknownst to all, in a plot twist straight out of *Riot on Sunset Strip*, she was also the daughter of the San Bernardino sheriff. Said sheriff, like practically all holding that office in 1966, policed on an anti-hippie, clean-up-the-town platform. In short order, he swore out arrest warrants for all the station's DJs. Peel felt he could have exonerated himself, but with a furious sheriff on his back, and with his travel visa long overstayed, he elected not to fight city hall. He left town within hours, eventually crossed into Canada as John Robert Parker, and returned to England.

Pirate

Back in his homeland, Peel longed for the free sounds he'd heard in California, but he found BBC radio to be totally, banally, out of touch. In another odd twist of fate, a neighbor in London knew someone who worked on the pirate radio ship Radio London. Along with pirate Radio Caroline, RL was illegally broadcasting a steady stream of pop and psychedelic music from a ship anchored five miles off the UK coast. He was hired to do Top 40 during the day, but also volunteered to pull the midnight-to-three shift, developing his unique programming style that would last close to four decades. "When I realized none of the management was listening at night, I did away with the format and played when I wanted, even read listeners' poetry—hippie stuff I would find amazingly embarrassing if I heard it now."

But the pirate era was ending. The British government whipped up draconian new laws granting them the power to board ships in international waters and confiscate gear and record collections in the name of national security. Peel's pirate stint lasted only five months. The BBC had seen their youth audience near-totally absorbed by the pirates and the Euro mega-power Radio Luxembourg, so reluctantly, the BBC created Radio 1 in 1967, signing on with The Move's "Flowers In The Rain." Even more reluctantly, the BBC was forced to turn to former pirate DJs to try to shore up some semblance of credibility. Among the first group of DJs hired, Peel would outlast them all, playing music on BBC Radio 1 continuously from 1967 to October 2004.

The Shock of the New

When punk arrived, Peel carried the torch for this amazing new wave of audacity and amateurism, finding it to be "a welcome breath of foul air. When I first played the Ramones, I got nasty letters from people wanting me to play the Grateful Dead for the rest of their lives. The average age of the audience in those four months dropped from 25 to 15." Peel's longtime producer John Waters once said, "When we were listening to new bands, it was like John had a divining rod . . . as if he'd walk out into the middle of a huge field and say, 'It's here.'"

In 1977, Peel was almost fired for playing the Sex Pistols on the BBC; in 1997, Peel's BBC show was pre-empted for a long-form Sex Pistols radio tribute special.

He was first to play a number of historic albums in their entirety, from *Sgt. Pepper's* to *Trout Mask Replica* to *Meat Is Murder*. Genres we are now all familiar with, from punk to gangsta to grunge and jungle, he played first before these genres even had a name.

Looking Back and Forward

I first wrote Peel nearly 20 years ago to just say thanks for the weekly BBC show he did on shortwave (with passable reception in Atlanta), and to mention that a band he'd played doing a punked-up Paul Simon cover was nothing new to Atlantans. I didn't expect a response, but he wrote back promptly. Apparently he didn't get much international mail at all for World Service shows other than "play-more-Hall-and-Oates" requests. So in the rare instance someone wrote to say they "got it," he took note.

In his reply he said I should "tell Danny Beard I played that Coolies record a lot." He also asked to send him any Atlanta and regional records he might enjoy. I sent off the 688 Records compilation (and he latched on to Dash Rip Rock briefly) and many other letters and records over time. Once, he replied to a comment I'd made about a great weird reggae record he'd played by, surprisingly, sending me a copy of the record he bought himself. This went on for years, and we'd meet for a pint whenever I'd visit London.

I was invited to his house in the English countryside, where I last saw him in 2001. It was a normal Saturday at "Peel Acres," and he was preparing for yet another week of shows. He seemed to spend every waking hour auditioning records, finding favor with perhaps 30% and discarding the rest.

I had always assumed these shows just rolled out before me for everyone's enjoyment as if by effortless magic. Now I knew better. By the end of that week, six more hours of blank run sheets stared back at him and it was time to start the process again.

Confidence

BBC Radio's daytime programs in the '80s, though pop-laden, were still filled with incredibly cheesy presentation and inane patter. Undaunted, Peel trudged on. As the tributes pour in now in late 2004, it's worth remembering this quote from 1987: "BBC Radio 1 is not sympathetic to my program and music. In 20 years, no one in the building has ever come in with an encouraging or complimentary word. In a way, it keeps you going; you say 'I'll show the bastards!'"

Peel told *Pulse Magazine* in 1990, "I can't understand why people want to hear stuff coming out of the radio that they've got on record at home and have heard a hundred times before!" There you have it: one voice, in one sentence, totally trashing the business model of corporate FM radio today.

John Peel had the fearless confidence that within one program it was totally logical to mix alt-country, cutting-edge dance, dub reggae, death metal, and African pop, alongside the most ragged yet earnest young bands. As Peel told *Stomp and Stammer* in

2000, "There's good stuff going on all the time." His program format was radically simple: say what you are about to play, play it, say what it was, even if it is 15 seconds of speedpunk. "Sometimes the music was just awful," said fellow BBC DJ Andy Kershaw. "But you mainly listened to Peel for Peel."

It has been estimated that 80% of the music he played in his 37-year run on the BBC had never been played on the radio before. And 98% of what he played, he played once and never again. Although an expert radio technician, he'd regularly play records at the wrong speeds, leaving him embarrassed but defensive. Look, he'd say, these are white label 12 inchers with no artist, titles, or speed info at all—but killer tracks nonetheless. It would be so much easier not to play them at all, and most DJs would do just that.

BBC Radio began webcasting in 1997, giving his extended domestic program an international reach. And soon ISDN technology enabled him to do his late-night programs from a small studio at his home in the country, a few steps from his astounding personal record library. Freed from the bureaucratic hassles of transmitting from BBC HQ, and elated at the instant feedback from both positive and negative e-mails, he had recently said he had never enjoyed presenting radio shows so much.

His impact on so many lives is immeasurable. Nearly every listener considered him a personal friend to some degree. And the few listeners that would contact him directly, such as this writer, found a lasting and real friendship. That friendship, like the man himself, will be irreplaceable.

Final Farewell

The massive 400-year-old St Edmundsbury Cathedral, near John's rural home of Stowmarket, was the setting for John's funeral on Nov. 12. Some 900 mourners had filled the church more than an hour before the service's start, while an overflow throng amassed before loudspeakers on the abbey lawn. There were hundreds of friends from the nearby villages and hundreds of BBC staffers, both young hip DJs and retired legendary voices going back to the birth of Radio 1. A swarm of British paparazzi camped outside the church zeroed in on the arrivals of Robert Plant, the White Stripes, Billy Bragg, Jarvis Cocker, Michael McCartney, and on and on.

Soon a sole church bell began tolling, and all fell silent.

John's casket, borne on the shoulders of six bleary-eyed pallbearers and piled high with Liverpool-red flowers, was carried from the hearse to the cathedral's center aisle. As the Stowmarket Choral Society gently sang, there came the heart-breaking sight of John's widow Sheila and his four grieving children, slowly followed the casket to the altar.

Amidst the somber mood, some of the eulogies were as funny as they were touching, but mostly the service was as sad as sad gets. Yes there were Bible readings and hymns, but also John's eclectic stamp was evident. At one point the hymns stopped, and across the vast cathedral space began the opening notes of the 1950s Howlin' Wolf classic "Goin' Down Slow," the Chicago blues masterpiece about one man's reflection on a life well-lived.

As Wolf's maniacal vocals bounced over the pews to the five stories of stained glass that surrounded us, I was filled with radically mixed emotions, unsure whether to laugh or cry. As the song ended, fading into a blurry ambient gauze, the more musically knowledgeable looked at each other and smiled broadly, while the villagers and the cheese-era BBC staffers seemed to be asking John yet again, "Just what was that awful racket??"

There was other music that day, from Mozart to Roy Orbison, and after these and after every eulogy, the church remained silent, while in the distance could be heard the roaring applause of the thousand-plus listening outside in the cold drizzle.

The concluding eulogy was co-written by John's four children, now in their teens and twenties, and read by a family friend. As they had entered that day it was clear they were emotionally wiped out, yet the tribute they had written was fresh, clever brash, bratty, insulting, and fun, just like pops.

Although John Peel had always admitted he was on an endless quest to find the perfect record, he had long ago decided that "Teenage Kicks" by Ireland's the Undertones was his favorite record of all time. "Sheila, my wife, knows that when I die, the only words I want on my tombstone, apart from my name, are: 'Teenage Dreams, So Hard to Beat.'"

As the cathedral doors were swung open, the pallbearers raised the casket and started back up the center aisle. The weeping congregation rose, and, not unexpectedly, the church was filled with the sound of "Teenage Kicks" played really, really loud. "I wanna hold you wanna hold you tight, Get teenage kicks right through the night, Oh yeah."

OTHER NOTABLE ESSAYS OF 2004

Alex Abramovich/Alex Ross, "Bob Dylan's *Chronicles, Vol. 1*" (*Slate*, October 18, 2004)
Carson Arnold, "Patti Smith: The Art of Trampin'" (*Longhouse*, April 24, 2004)
Greg Beato, "Too Old to Rock, Too Young to Die" (*LA Weekly*, March 12–18, 2004)
William Booth, "Heavy Metal" (*Washington Post Magazine*, March 7, 2004)
David Cantwell, "Farther Along: Ray Charles, 1930–2004" (*No Depression*, September/October 2004)
Jon Caramanica, "The End of Eminem" (*Village Voice*, November 30, 2004)
Daphne Carr, "Dance, Dance . . . Revolution?" (*Seattle Weekly*, Sept. 8–14, 2004)
Ta-Nehisi Coates, "Just Another Quick-Witted, Egg-Roll-Joke-Making, Insult-Hurling Chinese-American Rapper" (*New York Times Magazine*, November 21, 2004)
Erik Davis, "Cameo Demons: Sun City Girls" (*The Wire*, February 2004)
Francis Davis, "God's Lonely Man" (*Atlantic Monthly*, March 2004)
Baz Dreisinger, "Jamaica's New Music Revolution" (*Salon*, March 13, 2004)
Chuck Eddy, "Nashville Catches Up" (*Village Voice*, May 28, 2004)
Steve Erickson, "Paul Is Dead" (*Black Clock*, Fall/Winter 2004)
Bill Friskics-Warren, "Twilight Time" (*No Depression*, September/October 2004)
Gary Giddins, "Fresh Flowers for Albert" (*Jazz Times*, December 2004)
David Hajdu, "Unchained Heart" (*New Republic*, December 13, 2004)
Howard Hampton, "Build Me an L.A. Woman" (*Believer*, June 2004)
Dave Hickey, "*His Mickey Mouse Ways*" (*Texas Monthly*, June 2004)
Sean Howe, "There but for Grace Is God" (*Black Clock*, Fall/Winter 2004)
Mark Jacobson, "L.I.R.R. (Long Island Rock 'n' Roll)" (*New York*, December 13, 2004)
Monica Kendrick, "Going Back to Rockville" (*Chicago Reader*, November 5, 2004)
David Kirby, "Bang the Drum All Day" (*Cincinnati Review*, Fall 2004)
Chuck Klosterman, "A Ghost Story" (*Spin*, July 2004)

John Kruth, "Townes Van Zandt: The Self-Destructive Hobo Saint" (*Sing Out!*, Summer 2004)
Jonathan Lethem, "Otis Redding's Lonely Hearts Club Band" (*Black Clock*, Fall/Winter 2004)
Guy Maddin, "The Song Was You" (*Believer*, June 2004)
Melissa Maerz, "Why Don't We Do It on the Road?" (*Citypages*, July 7, 2004)
Michaelangelo Matos, "The Home of House" (*Chicago Reader*, August 20, 2004)
Devin McKinney, "The Great Crank" (*The American Prospect Online*, October 29, 2004)
Mitch Meyers, "What Can You Do That's Fantastic" (*Downbeat*, January 2004)
Mark Anthony Neal, "A Pillar of Soul: Ray Charles" (*Africana*, June 15, 2004)
Eric Pape, "Shook Ones" (*Spin*, July 2004)
Dave Queen, "Wasting Their Hate" (*Citypages*, August 11, 2004)
Ben Ratliff, "'Happening, and Meandering, a Burst at a Time" (*New York Times*, December 24, 2004)
Alex Ross, "Bjork's Saga" (*New Yorker*, August 23, 2004)
Roni Sarig, "My Band" (*XXL*, November 2004)
Tom Smucker, "The Joan Baez of Jazz" (*Village Voice*, June 1, 2004)
Nick Sylvester, "Daft Punk: Daft Club" (*Pitchfork*, January 28, 2004)
Dave Tompkins, "Return to the World as a Thought" (*Crunkster*, August 5, 2004)
Wells Tower, "Rhyme and Reason" (*Washington Post Magazine*, June 27, 2004)
David L. Ulin, "Boulevard of Broken Dreams" (*Black Clock*, Fall/Winter 2004)
Michael Ventura, "Damballah Rising: The Lost Miles Davis/Jimi Hendrix Sessions" (*Black Clock*, Fall/Winter 2004)
Elijah Wald, "Leroy Carr: The Bluesman Who Behaved Too Well" (*New York Times*, July 18, 2004)
Alec Wilkinson, "The Ghostly Ones" (*New Yorker*, September 20, 2004)
Wayne Wilson, "A Quarter of a Man" (*The Cincinnati Review*, Fall 2004)

LIST OF CONTRIBUTORS

Robert Christgau has been a rock critic since 1967 and a senior editor for the *Village Voice* since 1974. He has published five books based on his journalism: three *Consumer Guide* compendiums, *Any Old Way You Choose It* (Penguin 1973, now Cooper Square), and *Grown Up All Wrong* (Harvard University Press, 1998). He has received fellowships from the John Simon Guggenheim Foundation (1987) and the National Arts Journalism Program (2002) to study the history of popular music.

Michael Corcoran lives in Austin, Texas. His book "All Over the Map: True Heroes of Texas Music" is being published by University of Texas Press.

Dave Eggers is the author *How We Are Hungry*, *You Shall Know Our Velocity*, and *A Heartbreaking Work of Staggering Genius*, a 2000 finalist for the Pulitzer Prize. He is the editor of *McSweeney's*, a journal and book publishing outfit. In 2002 he founded 826 Valencia, a nonprofit writing lab and tutoring center for youth in San Francisco, Brooklyn, and Los Angeles.

Sasha Frere-Jones is a writer and musician who lives in lower Manhattan. He is a staff writer for the *New Yorker*, and has written for a variety of periodicals and newspapers since 1995.

Robert Hilburn is the *Los Angeles Times* pop music critic.

Jessica Hopper is a feminist writer living in Chicago, IL. She is a frequent contributor to *City Pages*, *Chicago Reader*, and *Punk Planet*, and is the editor of *Hit it or Quit it*. Her book of essays is forthcoming from Akashic Books.

Andrew Hultkrans is the author of *Forever Changes* (Continuum, 2003), one of the inaugural six volumes in the 33⅓ series on celebrated rock and soul albums. From 1998 through 2003, he was editor-in-chief of *Bookforum* magazine. Over the years, his journalism and criticism have appeared in *Artforum*, *Bookforum*, *Wired*, *Salon*, *21C*, *Filmmaker*, *Tin House*, *Cabinet*, and the pioneering cyberculture magazine *Mondo 2000*, where he was managing editor and columnist for three years in the early '90s. He is at work on a book about surveillance in America.

Greil Marcus is the author of *Lipstick Traces* (1989), *Like a Rolling Stone: Bob Dylan at the Crossroads* (2005), *The Dustbin of History* (1995), *The Old, Weird America* (1997), and with Sean Wilentz, the editor of *The Rose & the Briar: Death, Love and Liberty in the American Ballad* (2004). He lives in Berkeley.

Evelyn McDonnell is the pop culture writer at the *Miami Herald*. She is the author of two books, *Army of She: Icelandic, Iconoclastic, Irrepressible Bjork* and *Rent by Jonathan Larson*. She co-edited the anthologies *Rock She Wrote: Women Write about Rock, Pop and Rap* and *Stars Don't Stand Still in the Sky: Music and Myth*. A former senior editor at the *Village Voice* and associate editor at *SF Weekly*, her writing has appeared in numerous publications and anthologies, including *Ms.*, *Rolling Stone*, the *New York Times*, *Spin*, *Travel & Leisure*, and *Option*.

A former *Spin* staffer, **Chris Norris** is a New York–based freelance writer. Recent projects include *The Wu-Tang Manual* written with RZA of the Wu-Tang Clan.

The Onion is a satirical newspaper and website published in New York City, NY; Chicago, IL; Minneapolis, MN; San Francisco, CA; Denver, CO; Madison, WI; and Milwaukee, WI. It can be found on the web at www.theonion.com.

Camille Paglia is University Professor of Humanities and Media Studies at the University of the Arts in Philadelphia and is the author of five books, including the best-selling *Break, Blow, Burn* (Pantheon Books, 2005). She is a contributing editor at *Interview* magazine and has written innumerable articles on art, literature, popular culture, feminism, and politics for newspapers and magazines around the world. She has also lectured and appeared on television and radio extensively in the United States and abroad.

Ann Powers is a senior critic for *Blender* magazine, co-author of *Tori Amos Piece by Piece: A Portrait of the Artist*, and author of *Weird Like Us: My Bohemian America*. She has been a pop music critic for more than twenty years, since her teens. "Edelweiss" originated as part of the "Bookmarks" tiny book series, edited by Brian Goedde and Megan Purn and published by Seattle Research Institute.

David Ritz has autobios with BB King, Ray Charles, Etta James, Aretha Franklin, Smokey Robinson, the Neville Brothers and bios of Marvin Gaye and Jimmy Scott. His lyrics include "Sexual Healing." His most recent book is *Elvis by the Presleys*. He's won the Gleason Book Award four times.

Tom Roche has successfully crashed this literary cocktail party; he's actually a madly diverse filmmaker/editor in Atlanta. There's early R.E.M. video editing ("Finest Worksong"), concert videos as disparate as Norah Jones and Melt-Banana, and even 55 episodes of the pioneering *Space Ghost Coast-to-Coast* on his résumé. He's presently filming the documentary *Alley Pat: The Music Is Recorded* about 1950s Atlanta black radio. He writes only occasionally, purely for the huge amounts of money to be made.

Kalefa Sanneh writes about popular music for the *New York Times*. In response to the article republished in this book, one reader called him a "hipster Gene Shalit." He couldn't have put it better himself.

Luc Sante still possesses the thirty or forty rejection slips he collected from *Rolling Stone* between the ages of 14 and 16. He also has a Grammy, for album notes, and two songs he co-wrote appear on the soundtrack of Wim Wenders's *The State of Things*. His books include *Low Life*, *Evidence*, and *The Factory of Facts*. He teaches at Bard College.

David Segal was the rock critic at the *Washington Post* for four years. He is currently based in New York City, writing features for the paper's style section.

Ingrid Sischy is the editor-in-chief of *Interview* magazine, a position she has held since 1989. Prior to joining *Interview*, Sischy was the editor-in-chief of *Artforum* from 1979–1988, after which she joined the *New Yorker* as a staff writer and as the magazine's photography critic, later adding the title of fashion critic as well. Since 1997, Sischy has been a contributing editor of *Vanity Fair*, and she is also a frequent contributor to *The New York Times Magazine*.

Ben Yagoda is the author of *The Sound on the Page: Style and Voice in Writing*, *About Town: The New Yorker and the World It Made*, and *Will Rogers: A Biography*. He has written for the *New York Times Magazine*, *Slate*, *Esquire*, and many other publications. He directs the journalism program at the University of Delaware, and lives in Swarthmore, Pennsylvania, with his wife and two daughters. He is working on a book about the parts of speech.

Nicole White is a *Miami Herald* reporter who covers politics, nightlife, and cultural trends in the city of Miami Beach. Nicole, a Jamaican native, has worked as a general assignment reporter and covered the state legislative session for the *Herald*. She has also written freelance pieces for publications including *Vibe* and *Rhythm* magazines. Before joining the *Herald*, Nicole was a reporter for the *Journal News* in White Plains, New York, and an intern for the political section of the *Village Voice*. Nicole is the Vice-President/Print for the South Florida Black Journalist Association.

ACKNOWLEDGMENTS

I feel so very in awe of all the pieces contained within this book. A deep bow of appreciation to the writers within. And to the rights/permission-getting and -granting folks.

I read so many pieces that should be in here too, but they told me this is not a Bible . . . even though I started genuflecting to it. 'Twas a slow, painful process, but I get off on stuff like that . . . So my hearty gratitude extended to all them swell patient folks of Da Capo-ville. Especially Ben Schafer for his humor, friendship, patience, and the swell music sent my way.

Special thanks to Kate Kazeniac, Paul Bresnick, Marvelous editor God Michael Ray, Mary Gaitskill, Bruce Benderson, John Strausbaugh, Martha Keith, Doreen Remen and Art Production Fund, Litsa and Anna Dremousis and their feral world of art and baklava! Kelly Cutrone and People's Revolution, Kate Vukelic, Ben Foster, Charlie Wessler, Billie Fisher and Co., Shelley Marlow, Ira Silverberg, Anne Ystenes, Brian Young and Untitled Entertainment, Nicole Cimino and Pretty and Mean, Hollipops, Mike Potter, Eric Wilinski, and David Milch and *Deadwood*.

Thanks to the Stanford Inn and Spa in Mendocino, California, where I plopped amidst the redwoods, gorged on divine scones, and played Rock 'n' Roll Theology. And my eternal indebtedness to the Gary Graham Collections for fantasy made into wearable stories. Also the reading of this book was fueled by Scharffen Berger chocolate.

Last but not least, thanks to them publicists that didn't hang up on me, and even to those that did.

Got any swell music for me? Or dark chocolate? Or just wanna say howdy? Email me at le_terminator22@hotmail.com or www.JTLEROY.COM. Check out my band, THISTLE LLC., at www.THISTLEHQ.com.

And always, my gratitude, my love to Nancy Murdock, the rockinest fourth grade teacher around!

—JT LeRoy

CREDITS

"Editor Ingrid Sischy Talks to Camille Paglia" by Ingrid Sischy and Camille Paglia. Originally published in *Interview* magazine, August 2004, Brant Publications, Inc.

"1979 Calling" by Michael Corcoran. First published in the *Austin-American Statesman*, October 3, 2004. Copyright © 2004 *Austin-American Statesman*.

"In Search of Jim Crow" by Robert Christgau. First published in *Believer*, February 2004. Copyright © 2004 Robert Christgau.

"And Now, a Less Informed Opinion" by Dave Eggers. First published in the July 2004 issue of *Spin*. Reprinted with permission of the author. All rights reserved.

"1979: The Year Punk Died, and Was Reborn" by Sasha Frere-Jones. First published in the *New Yorker*, November 1, 2004. Used by permission of the author.

"Rock's Enigmatic Poet Opens a Long-Private Door" by Robert Hilburn. First published in the *Los Angeles Times*, April 4, 2004. Copyright © 2004 *Los Angeles Times*. Reprinted with permission.

"Punk Is Dead! Long Live Punk!" by Jessica Hopper. First published in the *Chicago Reader*, August 20, 2004. Copyright © Jessica Hopper.

"Revolution Blues" by Andrew Hultkrans. First published in *Black Clock* #2. Copyright © 2004 Andrew Hultkrans. All rights reserved.

"The Lost Boy" by Greil Marcus. First published in *Mojo*, October 2004. Copyright © 2004 by Greil Marcus. Used by permission.

"The Ghost of Saint Kurt" by Chris Norris. First published in the April 2004 issue of *Spin*. Reprinted with permission from *Spin* magazine. All rights reserved.

"Heartbreaking Country Ballad Paralyzes Trucking Industry" by the editors of *The Onion*. Copyright © 2004 Onion, Inc. All rights reserved. Reprinted with permission. www.theonion.com.

"Edelweiss" by Ann Powers. First published in the *Bookmarks* series published by Seattle Research Institute. Copyright © 2004 Ann Powers.

"The Last Days of Brother Ray" by David Ritz. First published in *Rolling Stone*, July 8–22, 2004. Copyright © 2004 Ritz Writes, Inc.

"The Rap Against Rockism" by Kalefah Sanneh. First published in the *New York Times*, October 31, 2004. Copyright © 2004 by The New York Times Co. Reprinted with permission.

"I Thought I Heard Buddy Bolden Say" by Luc Sante. First published in *Believer*, November 2004. Copyright © 2004 Luc Sante.

"The Shortwave and the Calling" by David Segal. First published in the *Washington Post*, August 3, 2004. Used by permission of the author.

"Police Secretly Watching Hip-Hop Artists" by Nicole White and Evelyn McDonnell. First published in the *Miami Herald*, March 9, 2004. Used with permission of Miami Herald Publishing Company.

"Heavy Meta" Copyright © by Ben Yagoda. This article originally appeared in *The American Scholar*, Summer 2004.

"There Is a Light That Never Goes Out" by Tom Roche. First published in *Stomp and Stammer*, December 2004. Copyright © 2004 by Tom Roche.